Cabinetmaking

KEN CALHOUN

*Associate Professor of Technology
and Industrial Education
Central Washington University*

PRENTICE-HALL, INC., *Englewood Cliffs, New Jersey 07632*

Library of Congress Cataloging in Publication Data

CALHOUN, KEN. (date)
    Cabinetmaking.

    Includes index.
    1. Cabinet-work.   I. Title.
TT197.C24 1984   684.1'6   83-19214
ISBN 0-13-110064-5

Cover photo courtesy of Ranier
    Woodworking Co., Puyallup, Washington
Editorial/production supervision and
    interior design by Tom Aloisi
Cover design by Mark Berghash
Manufacturing buyer: Anthony Caruso

Popular Science Book Club offers a wood identification kit that includes 30 samples of cabinet
woods. For details on ordering, please write:
Popular Science Book Club, Member Services,
P.O. Box 2033, Latham, N.Y. 12111.

Printed in the United States of America

10   9   8   7   6   5   4

ISBN: 0-13-110064-5

PRENTICE-HALL INTERNATIONAL, INC., *London*
PRENTICE-HALL OF AUSTRALIA PTY. LIMITED, *Sydney*
EDITORA PRENTICE-HALL DO BRASIL, LTDA., *Rio de Janeiro*
PRENTICE-HALL CANADA INC., *Toronto*
PRENTICE-HALL OF INDIA PRIVATE LIMITED, *New Delhi*
PRENTICE-HALL OF JAPAN, INC., *Tokyo*
PRENTICE-HALL OF SOUTHEAST ASIA PTE. LTD., *Singapore*
WHITEHALL BOOKS LIMITED, *Wellington, New Zealand*

Contents

PREFACE   vii

CHAPTER 1   INTRODUCTION TO CABINETMAKING   1

CHAPTER 2   CABINET DESIGN   3

Visual Design, *3*
Functional Design, *6*
Space Utilization, *10*

CHAPTER 3   CABINET MATERIALS   15

Classification of Trees, *16*
Wood Composition, *16*
Moisture, Shrinkage, and Expansion, *18*
Cabinetmaking Woods, *23*
Methods of Cutting Lumber, *28*
Lumber Grades, *29*
Lumber Sizes, *30*
Determining Lumber Quantities, *31*
Sheet Materials, *31*
High-Pressure Plastic Laminates, *36*

Adhesives, *37*
Fasteners, *38*
Cabinet Hardware, *41*
Abrasives, *48*
Summary, *48*

CHAPTER 4   CABINET TYPES AND CONSTRUCTION DETAILS   51

Base Cabinets, *51*
Wall Cabinets, *57*
Special Cabinets, *60*
Bath Cabinets, *63*

CHAPTER 5   DEVELOPING SHOP DRAWINGS FROM BLUEPRINTS   65

Building Plans, *65*
Shop Drawings, *66*
On-Site Measurements, *67*
Preparing Shop Drawings, *68*
The Cutting List, *78*

CHAPTER 6   MACHINING AND ASSEMBLING THE FACE FRAME   85

Sizing Rough Lumber, *86*
Cutting Face-Frame Parts, *88*
Layout for Machining, *91*
Machining Face-Frame Joints, *92*
Face-Frame Assembly, *99*

CHAPTER 7   CABINET DOORS   103

Types of Doors, *103*
Door Styles, *106*
Making Flat Doors, *109*
Making Frame-and-Panel Doors, *114*
Sliding and Tambour Doors, *127*

CHAPTER 8   DRAWERS AND DRAWER GUIDE SYSTEMS   129

Drawer Types and Styles, *129*
Drawer Design and Construction, *130*
Machining Drawer Joints, *131*

Drawer Assembly, *136*
Drawer Guide Systems, *138*
Roll-out Trays, *144*

CHAPTER 9   CABINET CUTOUT AND MACHINING   147

Measurements and Accuracy, *147*
Handling Sheet Materials on the Table Saw, *150*
Cutting Cabinet Parts to Size, *153*
Machining Operations, *157*
Machining Moldings, *162*
Machine Safety Guidelines, *169*

CHAPTER 10   CABINET ASSEMBLY   173

Assembling the Base Cabinet, *173*
Sanding the Cabinet, *185*
Installing Drawers, *187*
Hanging Doors, *188*
Assembling the Wall Cabinet, *188*

CHAPTER 11   FINISHING   195

Preparing the Wood for Finishing, *196*
Finishing Products, *197*
Finishing Equipment, *201*
Spray Finishing Techniques, *204*
Summary, *208*

CHAPTER 12   CABINET INSTALLATION   211

Setting Base Cabinets, *211*
Setting Wall Cabinets, *219*
Final Check, *221*

CHAPTER 13   INSTALLING PLASTIC LAMINATE COUNTERTOPS   223

Cutting Parts to Size, *223*
Applying the Edge Band, *225*
Applying the Top, *228*
Cutout for a Sink, *230*
Applying the Backsplash, *232*

CHAPTER 14   ESTIMATING AND BIDDING   235

Factors Involved in Pricing Cabinetwork, *235*
Shop Time Rates, *237*
Detailed Quantity-Takeoff Estimates, *237*
Unit Price Estimates, *239*
Reading Architectural Drawings and Specifications, *240*
Submitting the Bid, *241*
Getting Invited to Bid, *241*

INDEX   243

Preface

Residential cabinets range in quality from crude boxes using questionable construction techniques to elegant built-in furniture carefully constructed from the finest hardwoods with cost no object. However, the market for which most small to medium cabinet shops aim is between these two extremes. The purpose of this book is to show the reader how to build professional-quality cabinets while keeping labor and material costs to moderate levels.

This book is designed for use in apprenticeship programs, vocational and technical school programs, and college courses. It may also be used in upper-level senior high school courses. The hobby woodworker who would like to build cabinets will also find this book very helpful.

It is assumed that the reader possesses some basic woodworking skill and is familiar with the operation of common woodworking equipment. This book is devoted to one branch of woodworking, namely cabinetmaking, and while it presents information on machine operation and joint construction as they pertain to cabinetmaking, it does not contain the detailed step-by-step instruction that a novice woodworker may require. There are a number of basic woodworking books on the market for those who may need a review or further study in this area.

This book is oriented toward the construction of kitchen cabinets, although many of the techniques presented can be applied to cabinets for commercial buildings.

The first part of the book shows the reader construction and design details of typical cabinets. The second part takes the reader step by step through the construction, finishing, and installation of typical cabinets. The ability to produce a quality product at a reasonable price is stressed.

Most of the photographs that appear in this book were taken by Debbie Storlie, and I wish to express my appreciation for her work.

KEN CALHOUN

Ellensburg, Washington

Chapter 1

Introduction
to Cabinetmaking

Cabinetmaking, along with the related field of carpentry, dates back over several centuries. Unlike some of the emerging occupations, the field of cabinetmaking has many traditions, some of which are not compatible with the modern world. The word *cabinetmaker* often conjures up an image of an old man standing by a bench littered with shavings and an assortment of hand tools. He may be very patiently fitting two pieces of wood by putting them together, cutting a little from one piece, then putting them back together until they fit perfectly.

There are a number of things wrong with this image when viewed in light of today's reality. One of the first discrepancies is that the cabinetmaker in the above vision was a man. There are now many excellent women cabinetmakers. Another problem with that image is that it is no longer practical for someone to take hours to hand-fit parts when shop time may be $20 to $25 per hour and climbing rapidly. This does not mean, however, that quality workmanship is not important. As a matter of fact, one of the reasons that people have cabinets custom built is that they have become disillusioned with the quality of some lower-quality, mass-produced cabinets. However, this quality must be achieved through intelligent use of materials and accurate and efficient machining and assembly operations that minimize hand-fitting of parts.

Let's take a look at some of the things that a modern cabinetmaker is expected to be able to do. From a shop drawing of a set of cabinets, the cabinetmaker must be able to develop a cutting list, then quickly and accurately cut all parts to size from solid lumber and sheet materials as specified. He or she must then be able to do all the required machining operations necessary for making joints and for hardware installation. The parts must then be assembled into cabinets as specified and prepared for finishing. The cabinetmaker may also be required to finish the cabinets, install them, and install plastic laminate countertops.

In addition to these operations, the cabinetmaker may be involved in taking measurements on the job site, preparing shop drawings from blueprints, and preparing estimates and bids.

In order to do these things, the cabinetmaker must be able to read and interpret blueprints and must be familiar with cabinetmaking woods and with sheet materials such as plywoods, particle boards, medium-density fiberboards, hardboards, and plastic laminates.

Skill in operating a wide variety of woodworking machines is also very important. It is also necessary to be familiar with a number of other products used in cabinetmaking, such as adhesives, abrasives, hardware, fasteners, and finishes.

This book is designed to show the reader how to design, build, finish, and install kitchen and other cabinets, in an efficient manner.

While the emphasis of the book is on efficiency in producing custom cabinets, every effort must be taken to maintain a quality product. Competition is very keen in this field, and with rapidly escalating costs for material, labor, and utilities, it sometimes seems that the only way to cut or control costs is to reduce quality. However, if the cabinetmaker is alert to more efficient production methods, new developments in material, hardware, finishes, and machines, it is possible to maintain and even improve quality while controlling costs.

Chapter 2

Cabinet Design

VISUAL DESIGN

One of the first things that people notice when looking at cabinets is the style, or visual design, of the cabinets. A major part of this appearance is determined by the type of doors and drawer fronts used on the cabinet. The type of wood, finish, and hardware used also contribute greatly to the final appearance of the cabinet. Figure 2-1 shows some of the commonly used cabinet door and drawer front treatments.

The building owner will probably want the cabinets to match the general decoration theme of the house, so the cabinets may have to convey a colonial, Mediterranean, contemporary, or other theme. Owners of commercial buildings may be more interested in having smooth surfaces that are durable and easy to clean and to maintain than in having cabinets that are stylish.

Figure 2-2 shows cabinets with flat doors and drawer fronts. This is one of the most common types of door and drawer construction. It is very fast and easy to machine and easy to fit the doors and drawers. While not as stylish as some of the other types, it can be attractive, especially if the wood grain is matched on the door and drawer faces. It is usually associated with modern or contemporary design.

Figure 2-3 shows examples of frame and panel doors. These can be made in an almost endless variety of styles and can be very attractive. However, they are more costly to produce because they are made up of several parts that must be machined and assembled.

3

(a)

(b)

Figure 2-1 Door and drawer front styles greatly affect the appearance of the kitchen. (a) Courtesy of Roy Ricketts, Inc.; (b) Courtesy of Artstone, Inc.; (c, d, e) Courtesy of Rainier Woodworking.

(c)

(d)

(e)

Figure 2-2 Cabinets with flat doors

FUNCTIONAL DESIGN

Although appearance may be the first thing that people notice about a cabinet, its function is probably the most important aspect of its design. Rather than just filling the available space with an assortment of cabinets, careful thought should be given to the intended purpose of the cabinets.

Cabinets in a kitchen serve several functions. They must provide storage, appliance space, countertop work space, and, in some instances, dining space.

Storage must be provided for canned goods, various size package goods, dishes, eating utensils, serving utensils, pots and pans of various shapes, cleaning supplies, linens, and small portable appliances.

In addition to major appliances such as refrigerators, ranges, ovens, and dishwashers, there are many small appliances that must be accommodated. Those that are used frequently, such as can openers, toaster-ovens, food mixers, blenders, drip coffee makers, and even microwave ovens are frequently left on the counter. Unless adequate countertop space is provided, these appliances can seriously reduce the available working space. Occasionally an appliance, such as a mixer, is mounted on a special shelf that allows it to be stored inside the cabinet and then be pulled out and up to countertop height when needed.

The general layout of the kitchen is usually determined by the architect and is shown on the blueprints. From the blueprints, the cabinetmaker prepares accurate, detailed shop drawings showing construction details. These shop drawings are further described in Chapter 5.

Figure 2-3 Four of many possible frame and panel-style doors

(a)

(b)

(c)

(d)

However, the cabinetmaker is sometimes involved in planning the kitchen layout, especially in remodel construction. It is then necessary for the cabinetmaker to work with the home owner to determine a kitchen arrangement that will best meet the homeowner's needs.

Some people use the kitchen only for food storage, preparation, and cleanup. Others, however, may wish to include space for other activities such as dining, laundry, TV viewing, study, or office space for the homemaker. After the various needs have been ascertained, the cabinetmaker can begin to arrange cabinets and appliances into convenient locations that will facilitate these activities. Conventional kitchen planning calls for establishing "centers" for various tasks. A typical kitchen might contain a sink center, a mixing center, a cooking-serving center, and a refrigerator center. Each of these centers requires a certain amount of cabinet and countertop work space. The Small Homes Council, in conjunction with the University of Illinois,* has conducted extensive studies on the space requirements for these work centers. The space standards that they have established are proportional to house size and are specified as minimum standards for houses up to 1,000 sq. ft. in area, medium standards for houses between 1,000 and 1,400 sq. ft., and liberal standards for houses over 1,400 sq. ft. The suggested dimensions that follow are derived from these recommendations. The low end of the range represents the minimum standard, and the high end represents the liberal standard, which should be used when possible.

The sink center consists of the sink and its cabinet along with 24 to 36 in. of countertop on one side of the sink for dishes to be washed and 18 to 30 in. on the other side for drying dishes. A dishwasher may be incorporated in this center.

The mixing center is often combined with the refrigerator center. In either case, 36 to 42 in. of countertop space is recommended for the mixing center.

The refrigerator center consists of the refrigerator along with 15 to 18 in. of counter space on the latch side of the refrigerator for setting items being transferred to or from the refrigerator.

The cooking-serving center should have 15 to 24 in. beside the range for setting out serving dishes or plates and 15 to 18 in. beside the oven if it is a separate unit.

So far little mention has been made of the cabinet requirements for the various centers other than for the countertop space requirement. As a general rule, items should be stored at or near the point of first use. Sugar, flour, and baking powder and utensils such as mixing bowls, measuring cups, and rolling pin would be stored in the mixing area, for example. Cooking and serving equipment would be stored in the cooking-serving area, and so on.

The Farmers Home Administration (FHA) also has specific standards for countertop and cabinet storage space based on the number of bedrooms in the

*Courtesy of Small Homes Council—Building Research Council, University of Illinois at Urbana—Champaign.

house. Since many houses are financed with FHA guaranteed loans, it is important to meet these standards. They are available at local FHA county offices.

Before leaving the topic of space requirements, a word about general cabinet and appliance sizes is in order.

Typical kitchen cabinets include base cabinets, which are usually 36 in. high and 24 in. deep, and wall cabinets, which are usually 30 to 36 in. high and 12 in. deep. The recommended base cabinet frontage is 6, 8, and 10 ft. respectively for minimum, medium, and liberal standards. Frontage on sink cabinets is not counted, nor is "dead" corner-cabinet space.

Wall cabinets are usually placed 15 to 16 in. above the countertop to provide clearance for small appliances such as mixers. The recommended wall-cabinet frontage is the same as for base cabinets. This will provide for dinnerware storage for four people. If storage for service for 12 is desired, an additional 48 in. of wall-cabinet frontage should be provided.

Full wall-height storage cabinets are also sometimes used to provide additional storage. These may be quite shallow when space is scarce and can provide easy access to canned goods. Most major appliances come in standard sizes, so space requirements are fairly standard. However, extra-large sizes as well as compact sizes are available from some manufacturers, so the cabinet-maker should find out if a nonstandard appliance is going to be used before the final cabinet sizes are determined. If the kitchen layout is made before the appliances are purchased, the following allowances should be made: range, 30 1/2 in.; refrigerator, 36 in.; dishwasher, 24 1/2 in.; double sink, 36 in.; single sink, 24 in.; and built-in oven, 24 1/2 in.

The centers must now be arranged into a workable pattern. There are several basic kitchen layouts that are commonly used.

In the *one-wall kitchen* (Figure 2-4a), all cabinets and appliances are on one wall. This kitchen type is sometimes found in apartments, but it is not considered very efficient because of the excessive distance between appliances.

The *corridor kitchen* (Figure 2-4b) has its appliances and cabinets on two opposite walls. If properly designed with adequate space between opposite centers for doors to open, it can be quite efficient. There are no "dead" storage corners, as in L- and U-shaped kitchens. One drawback to the corridor kitchen design is that it often has a traffic pattern through the work area.

The *L-shaped kitchen* (Figure 2-4c) is quite often used when a dining area is preferred in the kitchen, since it leaves two walls available for this purpose. It is quite efficient and allows two people to work in the kitchen with less interference than some of the other designs.

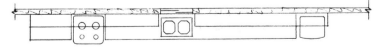

Figure 2-4-a One-wall kitchen

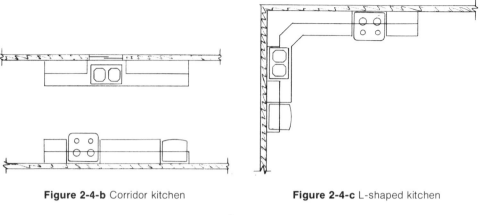

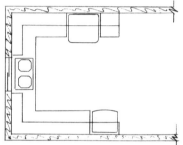

Figure 2-4-b Corridor kitchen

Figure 2-4-c L-shaped kitchen

Figure 2-4-d U-shaped kitchen

The *U-shaped kitchen* (Figure 2-4d) places all of the appliances in a compact work area and can result in a very efficient layout, usually best for only one person. It does have the disadvantage of having two corners, which tends to result in less efficient storage.

Whenever possible, the kitchen should be designed around a "work triangle" with the refrigerator, sink, and cooking-serving centers forming the points of the triangle. The total length of the three sides of this triangle should be between 23 and 26 ft. to be ideal. The U-shaped and corridor kitchens best lend themselves to achieving this ideal. Figure 2-5 shows several examples of work triangles.

SPACE UTILIZATION

The typical base cabinet has a countertop, a drawer under the top, and two fixed shelves, one of which is the cabinet bottom. This design, however, may not always be best for the items that are to be stored in the cabinet. The fixed shelf may not permit some items to stand upright or may allow too much wasted space. Since the base cabinet is usually 24 in. deep, it is also very difficult to reach items that are stored near the back of the bottom shelf.

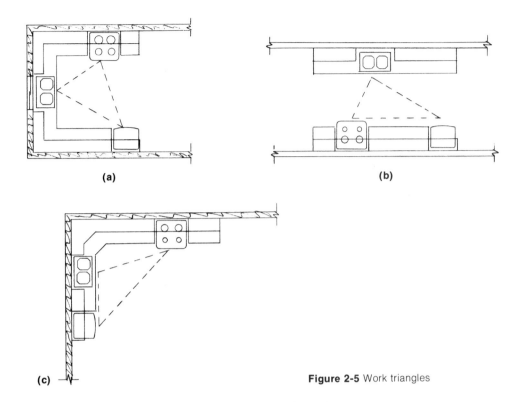

(a)   **(b)**

(c)   **Figure 2-5** Work triangles

Part of the space-utilization problem may be alleviated by making the shelf adjustable. Roll-out trays in place of shelves provide easy access to items stored in the back of the cabinet. These roll-out trays can also be mounted on special hardware that allows them to be adjusted for height (Figure 2-6).

Figure 2-6 Cabinet with roll-out trays rather than fixed shelves

Drawers provide more efficient storage for many items than do shelves. Consideration should be given to providing one or more banks or tiers of drawers in place of the usual single drawer and shelves.

Corner cabinets present a difficult space-utilization problem. In kitchens where space is at a premium, a Lazy Susan, or revolving shelves, may be incorporated into a corner cabinet to provide access to items stored in the corner (Figure 2-7).

A section of cabinet equipped with vertical dividers can provide space for flat items such as trays and cookie sheets (Figure 2-8).

Wall cabinets are usually equipped with adjustable shelves, which provide a great deal of flexibility in the types of items that may be accommodated.

Figure 2-7 Revolving shelves improve space utilization of corner cabinets. (Courtesy of Amerock Corporation)

Figure 2-8 Vertical dividers provide space for storing flat trays.

There are also a number of accessories available from hardware manufacturers that help to organize storage and increase space utilization. These include false-front trays used in the front of sink cabinets, flour and sugar bins, slide-out towel racks, various canned-goods racks, under-cabinet cookbook shelves, pull-out mixer shelves, and many others. Some of these are illustrated in Figure 2-9 (pp. 13–14).

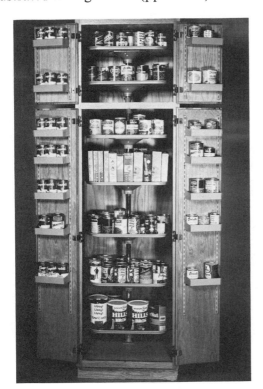

Figure 2-9 Typical convenience hardware designed to improve cabinet space utilization. (Courtesy of Amerock Corporation)

Figure 2-9 Continued

Chapter 3

Cabinet Materials

While there are many cabinets manufactured from metal and various plastics, wood is usually considered the most desirable material for residential and for many commercial cabinets. Our discussion of cabinet materials, therefore, will be limited to wood and wood-based products.

Wood has many advantages as a cabinet material. From the consumer's standpoint, it has an unequaled beauty and warmth. It is visually interesting, since no two pieces are exactly alike. It is available in an almost endless array of colors, textures, and grain patterns. It is very strong for its weight and is warm to the touch.

Wood also offers many advantages to the cabinetmaker. It is easy to cut and machine with general-purpose machines. In other words, it is not necessary to invest in sophisticated, special-purpose machines to produce wood parts. It is relatively easy to join parts, either with mechanical fasteners or adhesives. Wood is also relatively easy to finish.

In spite of all of these advantages, wood is not without its problems. It is subject to shrinkage, swelling, warping, and checking when subjected to different humidity levels. Not only do boards shrink as they dry, but they also shrink at different rates along each of their major axes (thickness, width, and length). Wood is also subject to a number of natural defects or limitations, such as knots, pitch pockets, and internal stresses. Woods of the same species may vary considerably in color and grain pattern, requiring selective matching in cabinet work. An understanding of the structure of wood is very helpful in solving these problems. A discussion of the composition and some of the properties of wood follows.

CLASSIFICATION OF TREES

Commercially useful woods are classified as softwoods if they are from coniferous trees and hardwoods if they are from deciduous trees. Coniferous, or cone-bearing, trees are evergreens and include such trees as Douglas fir, hemlock, the pines, and the cedars. Deciduous trees are broad-leafed trees that lose their leaves in winter and include such trees as the oaks, walnut, maple, and cherry. This may seem like a rather arbitrary system of classification, since some hardwoods are softer than some softwoods. However, there are some important differences in the wood structure of the two types. And though there are a number of exceptions, it is generally true that the wood from deciduous trees is harder than that from coniferous trees.

WOOD COMPOSITION

Wood is made up of many small cells. Tree growth occurs by cell division. The wood cells are formed in the cambium, a very thin layer, one cell thick, between the wood and the bark. Most of these cells are long and tubular and have pointed ends. They are cemented together with a substance known as lignin. Most of these cells are oriented vertically in the tree.

Examination of the cross section of a tree trunk shows the following features (Figure 3-1).

Bark: The new bark cells are also formed in the cambium layer, so the bark growth actually occurs from inside the tree. This new bark growth is known as the inner bark. The outer bark is formed as cells from the inner bark become dead or inactive. It is quite brittle and unable to stretch as the tree grows, so it cracks and eventually sloughs off. It does provide the tree with protection against insects and diseases. The cambium is the area in which this new growth occurs. Both bark and wood cells are formed in the cambium.

Sapwood: The wood cells formed in the cambium layer become sapwood, the lighter-colored wood near the bark. These cells are active in conducting and storing sap for the tree and are considered to be the living part of the wood.

Heartwood: The darker center area of the tree is known as the heartwood. It is made up of cells that are technically dead or no longer active in the life process of the tree. The darker color is caused by resins, tannins, and other chemical materials deposited in the cells.

Although the sapwood has most of the same strength properties as the heartwood, it is usually less desirable as a cabinet wood because of its lack of coloring. The colors that we usually associate with the fine cabinet and furniture woods are the heartwood colors. For example, the sapwood of black

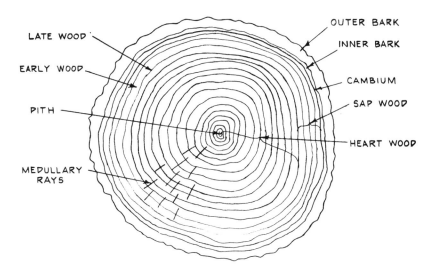

Figure 3-1 Tree cross section

walnut wood is a very light yellow brown rather than the desirable rich brown of the heartwood. The heartwood is also more resistant to decay because of the resin deposits.

Pith: The pith is the center of the trunk. It is rather soft and pronounced in some trees, and almost invisible in others.

Growth Rings: The wood cells formed early in each growing season are relatively large and have thin walls, resulting in a relatively soft wood known as earlywood or springwood. As the growth rate slows later in the summer, the cells formed are smaller and the cell walls thicker. This results in a harder, denser wood known as latewood or summerwood. This darker ring of summer wood is known as the growth ring. The growth rings can be counted to find the age of the tree. The rings are usually most pronounced in trees that are grown in climates with distinct growing seasons. Wood grown in more temperate climates has growth rings, but they are very difficult to see. Growth rings form the characteristic grain patterns seen in all woods.

Medullary Rays: The medullary rays are cells that are oriented horizontally in the tree and serve the purpose of conducting food laterally in the tree. They radiate from the center of the tree and exist in all woods. In softwoods, these rays are only one cell thick and are visible only with very high magnification. On the other hand, many hardwoods such as oak have very prominent rays, which provide the wood with some of its characteristic markings. These rays are especially noticeable as large flecks on a radial cut as shown in Figure 3-2.

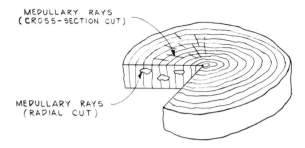

MEDULLARY RAYS
(CROSS-SECTION CUT)

MEDULLARY RAYS
(RADIAL CUT)

Figure 3-2 Medullary rays

Microscopic Features of Wood: Other important features of wood require magnification for study. An end-grain surface of a hardwood has many small openings known as pores or vessels. These pores are visible without magnification on some woods such as red oak. In some woods, these pores are larger in the spring wood and appear to follow the growth ring. Such woods are known as ring-porous. Woods that have pores more uniformly distributed are known as diffuse-porous. This factor is useful in identifying certain woods.

There are several types of wood cells, but most of them are long, thin, tubular structures with pointed ends. Figure 3-3 shows a cross section of a group of wood cells.

The cell walls are made up of very small strands called microfibrils. These microfibrils are the smallest visible wood element and require the most powerful magnification in order to be seen. The microfibrils are made of cellulose, the basic wood substance, and lignin, an adhesivelike substance.

The lumen, or cell cavity, may contain water or some of the chemical materials mentioned earlier.

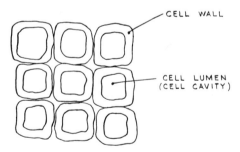

CELL WALL

CELL LUMEN
(CELL CAVITY)

Figure 3-3 Cross section of a group of wood cells

MOISTURE, SHRINKAGE, AND EXPANSION

One of the major problems faced by people building wood cabinets is that wood is not a dimensionally stable material. If a wood product is placed in a very dry environment, it will shrink. If it is placed back in a humid environment, it will expand. To compound the problem, a wood board will shrink and expand at very different rates along its three axes (thickness, width,

Figure 3-4 Moisture meter used to check the moisture content of a piece of wood

length) depending upon how it was cut from the log. Some of the problems that are caused, at least in part, by moisture are warping, checking, cracking, and joint failure due to expansion and contraction.

Wood is a hygroscopic material in that it readily absorbs moisture in liquid and vapor form. It may actually absorb in excess of twice its weight in water. The amount of water in the wood is referred to as moisture content and is expressed as a percentage of the oven-dry weight of the wood sample. Thus, a board that weighed 2 lb. before being completely dried in an oven to a dry weight of 1 lb. would have had a moisture content of 100%. A board that weighed 1 1/2 lb. wet and 1 lb. dry would have had a 50% moisture content, and so forth. Moisture meters (Figure 3-4) are available for checking moisture content. The moisture content of a sample piece of wood may also be found by weighing it accurately and then drying it in an oven at 200° F until it stops losing weight, weighing it again, and applying the following formula:

$$\text{Moisture content (\%)} = \frac{\text{Wet weight} - \text{Oven-dry weight}}{\text{Oven-dry weight}} \times 100$$

The ideal moisture content for cabinet woods varies somewhat from one region of the country to another, depending on relative humidity, but usually it is between 6% and 8%. Wood should be dried to 6% to 7% for dry regions and 8% to 9% for humid regions.

When a dry sample of wood is placed in a humid environment, it quickly begins to absorb moisture. The first water to enter the wood is absorbed in the cell walls. This absorption causes the microfibril strands to expand. Eventually a point is reached where the cell wall is completely saturated and any additional water entering the cell is taken into the lumen or cell cavity. This is known as the *fiber saturation point;* it occurs at about 25% to 30% moisture content in most woods.

The water absorbed in the cell walls is known as *bound water*, and the water stored in the cell cavities is known as *free water*. Once the fiber saturation point is reached, maximum cell expansion has occurred, and the addition of more water will make the sample heavier but will not cause additional expansion. This sequence is reversed in drying lumber. When wood is dried from the wet, or "green," condition, the free water leaves first. After the free water is gone, the bound water in the cell walls is given up. Cell shrinkage starts when the wood is dried below the fiber saturation point. In theory, we could have a board with 100% moisture content and dry it to 30% moisture content (just above the fiber saturation point) with no shrinkage. However, in practice, this seldom happens because moisture travels through the board slowly; the moisture content of cells near the surface of the board may be well below the fiber saturation point while cells in the center are well over 30% moisture content. This brings up another problem. Moisture moves much faster along the grain than it does across the grain because of the tubular cell structure. Therefore, the ends of a board, if not sealed, will dry much faster than the center of the board. The rapid shrinkage of these cells relative to the cells in the center of the board causes the familiar cracks and checks often seen at the ends of boards.

Wood cells shrink very little in length, but they shrink considerably in diameter. Consequently, the lengthwise shrinkage of most boards is negligible, but the shrinkage in thickness and width must be taken into account. There is also a significant difference in the shrinkage rate in a radial direction (perpendicular to the growth rings) as compared with a tangential direction (tangent to the growth of rings). Figure 3-5 illustrates this.

Radial shrinkage ranges from 2% to 6% for various woods dried to 6% moisture content, and the tangential shrinkage will be about twice that value. Thus, if we compare two boards of the same width (Figure 3-6), board A, which is cut tangentially from the tree, will shrink twice as much in width as board B, which is cut radially.

Also, board A, will tend to cup away from the center of the tree, as shown in Figure 3-7.

Since the shrinkage rate is different along the grain than across it, any major deviation in grain direction, such as that found around a knot, will tend to make a board bow or warp as it shrinks.

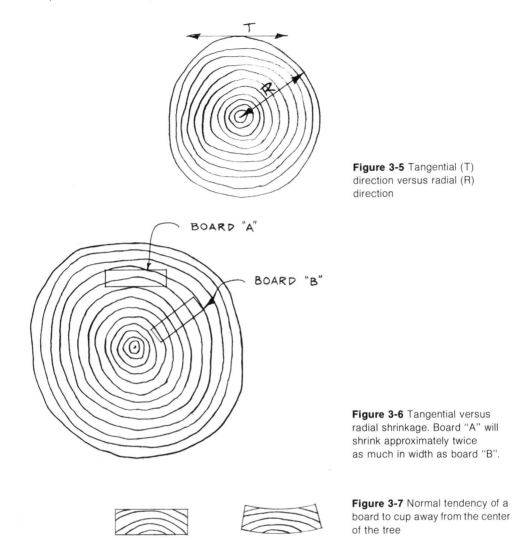

Figure 3-5 Tangential (T) direction versus radial (R) direction

BOARD "A"

BOARD "B"

Figure 3-6 Tangential versus radial shrinkage. Board "A" will shrink approximately twice as much in width as board "B".

Figure 3-7 Normal tendency of a board to cup away from the center of the tree

So far we have painted a rather gloomy picture of the problems that may be expected when working with wood. However, everyone who has worked with wood has had to face the same problems, and a number of techniques have been developed to eliminate many of these problems.

Storing and Handling Wood: One important consideration is to make sure that the moisture content of the wood has stabilized before you start working with it. If you started working the wood at 9% moisture content and it then dried to 7% moisture content, you would almost certainly have problems with warping and possibly checking. If you are building cabinets for a house in a relatively dry geographic area, for example, the moisture content of the wood should be 6% to 7%.

Wood should not be laid directly on the floor, where it can draw moisture. It should be stacked flat and well supported so that it is not allowed to sag or twist. Boards should not be leaned against an outside wall during the winter as there is a chance of drawing moisture.

Working with Wood: When working with solid lumber, a number of techniques may be used to prevent warpage. When gluing boards to make wide surfaces, it is best to cut the boards into narrow widths (1 1/2 to 3 in.) and glue these rather than gluing wide boards. The growth rings should be alternated as shown in Figure 3-8.

Figure 3-8 Direction of growth rings should be alternated when edge-gluing boards.

Any wide laminated wood surfaces should be attached to the final structure in a way that will allow them to expand and contract. Thus, a tabletop should be attached to the rails with blocks of wood as shown in Figure 3-9 rather than glued solidly in place. The panel in a frame-and-panel door should not be glued solidly in the frame but should only have a small spot of glue in the center, as shown in Figure 3-10, to hold it in place. This will allow the panel to expand without breaking the frame joints.

Drawer bottoms made of solid wood should not be glued in place for the same reasons.

Applying a finish to the wood will retard the rate at which wood absorbs and loses moisture but will not totally prevent it. All surfaces, including unexposed areas, should be finished on solid wood to prevent an uneven rate of moisture change. For example, a tabletop that is finished only on the top

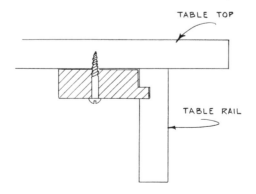

TABLE TOP

TABLE RAIL

Figure 3-9 Method of attaching a tabletop to allow for expansion and contraction

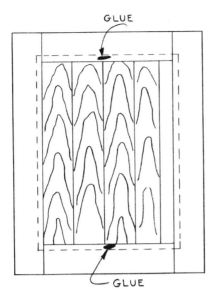

Figure 3-10 Glue applied to the center of a door panel to allow it to expand and contract

surface will absorb moisture rapidly through the bottom surface and will tend to warp.

Shrinkage and swelling are not the only problems caused by the moisture content of wood. The strength of wood increases as it is dried below the fiber saturation point. Nail and screw holding power is also increased. Successful wood gluing and finishing both require low moisture levels in the wood. Also, wood that is above 20% moisture content is subject to attack by fungi.

For these reasons, it is very important that wood be properly dried before being used for cabinetwork. Commercially available lumber is either air-dried or kiln-dried. Lumber may be air-dried down to about 20% moisture content in most climates. However, lower moisture-content levels are possible only under favorable climate and temperature conditions. The use of drying kilns allows very accurate control of moisture and allows the wood to be dried down to the desired 6% to 8% moisture-content level.

Obviously, kiln-dried lumber should be specified for all cabinetwork.

CABINETMAKING WOODS

Hundreds of woods are used commercially for lumber and veneers for various purposes. Many of these can and have been used for cabinetmaking. However, there are relatively few woods that are used in large quantities for cabinetmaking. Red oak and birch are two of the traditionally popular woods for residential cabinets. White oak, Philippine mahogany, cherry, white ash, alder, black walnut, maple, and pecan are all used to some extent; so are some softwoods, such as Douglas fir and several of the pines.

Characteristics of some of the most popular cabinet woods are described below.

Birch: (Figure 3-11): A dense, fairly heavy, hardwood, birch has a number of characteristics that make it one of the most popular of cabinet woods. It machines well and accepts stains and finishes well. It has very small pores and, when finished, has a uniform hard surface that is easy to clean. The heartwood is a light reddish brown, and the sapwood is a yellowish white. Birch is also readily available in plywood in select white (all sapwood), select red (all heartwood), or unselect (a mixture of heartwood and sapwood).

Red Oak (Figure 3-12): This wood is very hard, fairly heavy, and strong. It is ring-porous, and the pores are quite large and easily visible without magnification, as are medullary rays. The heartwood is a light red to pink in color, and the sapwood is a yellowish white. The grain pattern is usually quite prominent. Oak cabinets are very durable and attractive.

White Oak (Figure 3-13): White oak is somewhat similar to red oak in appearance, although its color tends to be a yellowish brown. It also has large pores, but they are not quite as visible since they are filled with a material called tyloses. White oak is usually somewhat more expensive than red oak. It is also very hard and durable.

Philippine Mahogany (Figure 3-14): A number of wood species are sold as Philippine mahogany. They are all relatively soft, very open-grained woods. They range in color from a very light pinkish white to a deep reddish brown. They are relatively inexpensive, and they machine easily. They accept stain readily, but because of their porous nature they usually require a paste wood filler if a smooth finish is to be obtained.

Hard Maple (Figure 3-15): A very dense, very hard wood, hard maple is diffuse-porous, with a very fine texture and grain. The heartwood is very light brown and the sapwood nearly white. It is somewhat difficult to machine as it tends to chip or tear out if machined against the grain. Because of its fine, dense grain and its hardness, it is an excellent wood for cutting-boards.

Black Walnut (Figure 3-16): This is the aristocrat of the American cabinet and furniture woods and is one of the most expensive. It has a very rich, dark brown heartwood with a light yellowish brown sapwood. It is an excellent machining wood with a fine, fairly uniform texture.

Alder (Figure 3-17): Until fairly recently, alder was used primarily as a firewood. However, it has found wide commercial acceptance in recent years and is often used in cabinetmaking. It is a light, fairly uniform brown wood, somewhat similar in appearance to the heartwood of birch, although it is much

Figure 3-11 Birch

Figure 3-12 Red oak

Figure 3-13 White oak

Figure 3-14 Philippine mahogany

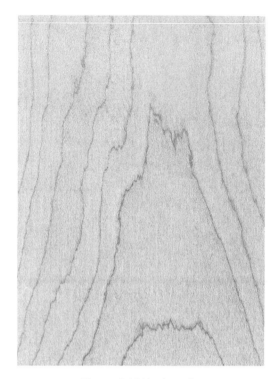

Figure 3-15 Hard maple

Figure 3-16 Black walnut

Figure 3-17 Alder

Figure 3-18 Cherry   **Figure 3-19** White ash

softer. It is quite often used for face frames on birch cabinets. It has a uniform texture and machines easily. It accepts stain well and is often used to imitate more costly woods.

Cherry (Figure 3-18): Cherry is an excellent furniture wood that is sometimes used for cabinetmaking. It is quite expensive but has very attractive coloring and grain patterns. The heartwood is predominantly a reddish brown, but traces of other colors such as green sometimes appear. The sapwood is a yellowish white. It is a nice machining wood, although it does tend to get burn marks if the wood is not moved past the cutters at a uniform speed or if the cutters are dull.

White Ash (Figure 3-19): A very hard, strong wood, white ash has the capability to withstand shock loads well, which makes it popular for baseball bats and handles for axes and hammers. It is occasionally used in cabinet-making. It is a very open-grained wood that is a very light yellow brown in color. It has a slight resemblance to certain oaks but does not have oak's highly visible medullary rays.

METHODS OF CUTTING LUMBER

The way in which a log is sawn into boards determines the appearance of the boards and also determines the shrinkage and strength characteristics of the boards. Figure 3-20 shows the most common method, known as plain sawing. Plain sawing is the least expensive method and results in the least waste. Figure 3-21 shows the quarter-sawn method, in which the log is quartered and then the boards are cut perpendicular to the growth rings. This method is considerably more expensive than the plain-sawn method and results in more waste material. However, the boards are less likely to shrink in width and tend to be more stable.

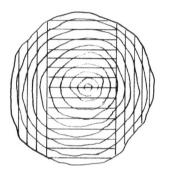
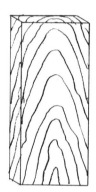

Figure 3-20 Plain-sawn lumber

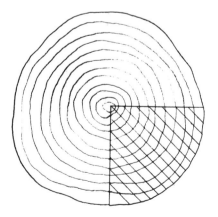
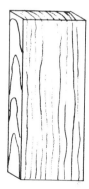

Figure 3-21 Quarter-sawn lumber

LUMBER GRADES

Lumber is a natural product, and no two boards are exactly alike. Many boards have characteristics that limit their usefulness for certain applications. A board may have a large knot, causing a weak spot that would render the board useless for structural applications. Another board may have a fungus stain that detracts from its appearance but would have no effect on its strength. Because of these and other problems, it has been necessary to develop a fairly complex system of grading boards based on their expected use so that the purchaser is assured of getting a product that will do the intended job. Traditionally, most softwood lumber has been used in fairly large boards for structural applications such as framing buildings, while hardwoods have been cut into smaller pieces for remanufacture into furniture and cabinets. Therefore, many of the softwood grades are based on the assumption that the entire board is to be used in one piece, and a large knot would downgrade the entire piece. Hardwoods, on the other hand, are usually graded on the percentage of usable wood (or clear cuttings) in a board, so a large knot would not necessarily be a serious defect in an otherwise clear board.

The actual grading specifications, in most cases, are developed by associations of lumber manufacturers. There are many grading classifications for various species of wood, and some of them are quite complex. It is not necessary for the cabinetmaker to have a thorough understanding of all the grading rules to make an intelligent selection of lumber. Of the multitude of grades and types of lumber available, only a few are intended for remanufacture into cabinets and millwork. A brief description of some of these grades follows.

Softwood Grades: Softwood lumber is generally classified according to *use*, *degree of manufacture*, and *size* for grading purposes.

Under the *use* classification, there are three categories: *yard lumber*, which includes light framing lumber; *structural lumber*, which is stress-rated for heavy framing; and *factory or shop lumber*, which is intended for remanufacture. This factory or shop category is of most interest to the cabinetmaker, since this lumber is intended to be remanufactured into such articles as sash and doors, cabinets, and other millwork. Shop lumber is usually sold S2S (surfaced two sides) in the following thicknesses:

4/4 S2S to 25/32 in.
5/4 S2S to 1 5/32 in.
6/4 S2S to 1 13/32 in.
8/4 S2S to 1 13/16 in.

Unlike softwood lumber intended for building construction, shop-grade lumber is graded on the basis of the number of usable cuttings that can be obtained from a board. The top grade of 4/4 (1 in.) shop lumber is called *factory select* (No. 3 clear) and must yield 70% or more clear cuttings of specified sizes. (Some typical sizes are 9 1/2 in. wide by 18 in. long and 5 in. wide by 3 ft. long.) *No. 1 shop* is the next grade and must yield between 50% and 70% clear cuttings (allowing some smaller cuttings). *No. 2 shop* must yield not less than 33 1/3% clear cuttings.

Hardwood Grades: The cabinetmaker is probably more concerned with hardwood grades than with softwoods. Fortunately, the grading system is less confusing. The grades that are most readily available are firsts and seconds (combined as one grade and abbreviated FAS), No. 1 common, and No. 2 common. Although the actual specifications for each grade are quite complex, one may assume that the FAS grade is approximately 90% usable, No. 1 common approximately 66.7% usable, and No. 2 common approximately 50% usable. There are also several other grades, but they are seldom sold.

LUMBER SIZES

Lumber is available rough-sawn, S2S (surfaced two sides) or S4S (surfaced four sides). Hardwood lumber is quite often purchased rough-sawn in 1- or 2-in. thicknesses and random widths. It is also usually available in S2S form, in which case 1-in. lumber is surfaced to either 13/16 in. or 25/32 in. This lumber is intended for eventual use at 3/4 in. thickness for face frames or door frames. While 1 in. and 2 in. are the most common thicknesses, others are available. These are sometimes listed by quarters: 4/4 in., 5/4 in., 8/4 in., and so on. Five-quarter lumber surfaced to 1 1/16 in. is often used for stair treads, for example. Softwood lumber in the factory or shop grade is also often surfaced 25/32 in. for remanufacture into cabinet and furniture parts or moldings. However, most softwood lumber is surfaced four sides to standard thicknesses and widths. Table 3-1 shows the nominal and finished dimensions of dry-planed softwood lumber.

Table 3-1 Nominal and Finished Sizes of Planed Lumber

Thickness		Width	
Nominal	Planed	Nominal	Planed
1 in.	3/4 in.	2 in.	1 1/2 in.
2 in.	1 1/2 in.	4 in.	3 1/2 in.
		6 in.	5 1/2 in.
		8 in.	7 1/4 in.
		10 in.	9 1/4 in.
		12 in.	11 1/4 in.

DETERMINING LUMBER QUANTITIES

Planed softwood lumber sold through retail outlets is usually sold by the linear foot. Most other lumber is sold by the board foot, quite often in 1,000 bd. ft. units. The board foot is a volume measurement: 1 bd. ft. is equal to 144 cu. in. of wood. The so-called standard board foot is 1 in. thick, 12 in. wide, and 12 in. long (144 cu. in.). Any combination of thickness, width, and length resulting in 144 cu. in. is 1 bd. ft. A board 2 in. by 6 in. by 12 in., a board 1 in. by 1 in. by 144 in., and a board 1 in. by 6 in. by 24 in. each contains 1 bd. ft. To calculate the number of board feet in a given board, the three dimensions of the board, expressed in inches, must be multiplied to give the number of cubic inches. To convert this to board feet, merely divide by 144. Thus, the formula is

$$\frac{\text{T in.} \times \text{W in.} \times \text{L in.}}{144} = \text{Bd. ft.}$$

where T = thickness in inches, W = width in inches, and L = length in inches. If the length is expressed in feet, the total is divided by 12 as follows:

$$\frac{\text{T in.} \times \text{W in.} \times \text{L ft.}}{12} = \text{Bd. ft.}$$

When estimating the number of board feet of lumber in a cabinet for the purpose of purchasing material, applying the formula to the various parts of the cabinet will only give the number of board feet in the finished product. This does not make allowance for cutting and planning parts to size. The amount of extra material required will vary greatly, depending on how efficiently the sizes can be cut from the rough boards. The actual extra amount that must be purchased will probably be at least 25% and may be much higher.

SHEET MATERIALS

Plywood: Plywood is a sheet material designed to take advantage of the fact that wood is very strong in the direction of the grain and that it shrinks very little in that direction. It is made by gluing alternate layers of wood at right angles to one another. Consequently, the strength properties tend to be more nearly equal across the width and length of the sheet. It also tends to be more stable than solid boards.

This construction gives plywood a number of other properties that make it especially useful as a cabinetmaking material. Unlike solid lumber, it has no tendency to check and split near the ends, even when nails are driven near the end. It is available with a number of attractive wood veneers on the surface. One of its biggest advantages as a cabinet material is that it is available presanded in large sheets and is ready to be cut to finished sizes. This saves many hours of work when compared with gluing solid boards together to make cabinet parts. Hardwood plywood is usually used for finished ends, finished backs, and sometimes for cabinet doors, drawer fronts, and shelves. Softwood plywood is usually used for cabinet backs and sometimes for drawer bottoms.

Softwood plywoods are usually available in 1/4-in., 3/8-in., 5/8-in., 3/4-in., and 1 1/8-in. thicknesses in sheets 4 ft. by 8 ft.

Hardwood plywoods are available in 1/4 in., 3/8 in., 1/2 in., and 3/4 in., with the 1/4-in. and 3/4-in. sizes the most readily available.

The veneers that make up softwood plywood sheets are graded for appearance using the letters A, B, C, D, and N according to standards developed by the American Plywood Association. N is a special grade for natural finish with no defects. In practice, it is rarely available. A is the next-best grade and allows a certain number of neatly made repairs. D is the lowest grade, permitting a number of open knots and other defects. A sheet labeled A-D would have a good surface on the A face and a number of exposed defects on the D face and thus would be suitable for exposure only on one side. Softwood plywoods are also classified as being interior type or exterior type. The two major factors determining whether a sheet is rated interior or exterior are the types of adhesives used (exterior type requires a waterproof adhesive) and the quality of veneer used. An exterior sheet of plywood cannot have a D-grade veneer on the surface or in the core. Much interior-type plywood is manufactured with waterproof adhesives, but because D-grade veneers are used, it cannot be sold as exterior plywood and will not meet building code requirements for exterior applications.

Hardwood plywoods use a numbered grading system for grading the veneers except for the premium grade (A). The grades and their general requirements are listed here:

- *Premium grade (A):* Only very minor defects permitted. Any edge joints must be tight and must be matched for grain and color.
- *Good grade (1):* Edge joints must be tight but color and grain matching are not required. Sharp color or grain contrasts are not permitted.
- *Second grade (2):* Veneer must be free of open defects. Grain and color matching is not required.
- *Utility grade (3):* Open defects are permitted.
- *Backing grade (4):* Similar to grade 3 but allows larger and more open defects.

Plywoods graded A-2 are often used for cabinet finished ends, while A-3 is often used for backs and drawer bottoms where only one side is exposed. Hardwood plywoods are also type-graded, based on their ability to withstand moisture exposure. Type I is waterproof; types II and III have progressively less resistance to moisture.

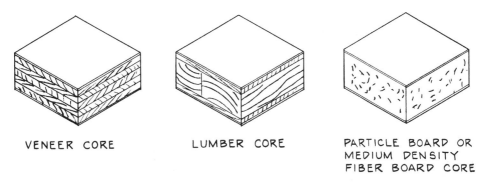

VENEER CORE   LUMBER CORE   PARTICLE BOARD OR
                                          MEDIUM DENSITY
                                          FIBER BOARD CORE

Figure 3-22 Plywood construction

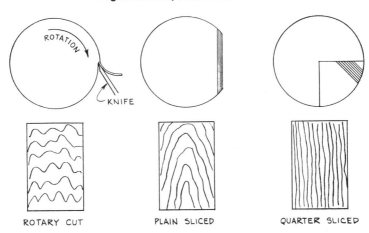

ROTARY CUT   PLAIN SLICED   QUARTER SLICED

Figure 3-23 Three common veneer-cutting methods and resulting grain
patterns

The core in hardwood plywoods may be constructed in one of three basic methods. These include veneer core, lumber core, and particle board (or medium-density fiberboard) core. These are shown in Figure 3-22.

Veneers for both hardwood and softwood plywoods may be cut from logs by a number of methods, three of which are shown in Figure 3-23. The method used determines the appearance of the veneer and affects the cost of the plywood sheet. Rotary-cut veneer is usually the least expensive. This process involves mounting the log in a large lathe and rotating the log while a long knife blade is used to peel a continuous layer of veneer from the log, much like unrolling a roll of paper towels. The veneer comes off in a continuous roll and is then cut to desired widths.

Flat or plain slicing is somewhat more expensive and involves slicing successive layers of veneer from the log. Adjacent layers of veneer are then edge-matched when used on the face of premium-grade panels. Quarterslicing is the third, and most expensive, of the popular veneer-cutting methods. It

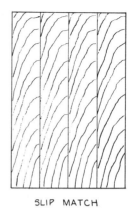

BOOK MATCH   SLIP MATCH

Figure 3-24 Two common methods of veneer matching for plywood

involves cutting the log into quarters and then slicing the veneer layers perpendicular to the growth rings. These layers again are kept in sequence and matched across the face of the plywood panel.

Several other veneer-cutting methods are sometimes used to take advantage of the characteristics of certain woods, but such veneers are usually only available on special order.

Veneers may be matched using a book match, in which successive veneers are opened up as a book would be opened, or they may be slip-matched, in which case the figure is repeated with each sheet (Figure 3-24).

These two methods are usually used for veneer matching on plywood sheets. Occasionally, however, the cabinetmaker may wish to obtain a special effect using veneer matches not available in plywood. Matched sets of veneers called flitches are available; the cabinetmaker can glue these to another surface

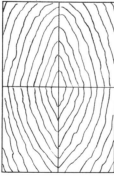
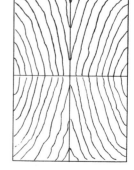

DIAMOND MATCH   REVERSE DIAMOND

Figure 3-25 Two common veneer-matching methods

(usually particle board or plywood) to achieve the desired effect. Two popular veneer-matching methods, known as the diamond match and the reverse diamond match, are shown in Figure 3-25.

In practice, veneer matching involves cutting the veneers with straight edges and then edge-gluing the veneers together. These pieces are held together with tape until they are glued to the substrate with a wood glue and a veneer press. If a veneer press is not available, contact cement may be used. Needless to say, this is a very exacting process and requires considerable practice.

Particle Board: Particle board is a manufactured sheet product made from wood chips bonded together with an adhesive. It is an engineered product, designed for a number of different applications. The two most readily available types are the underlayment type and the industrial type. The underlayment type is designed for use for floors under carpet or resilient floor coverings and should not be used for cabinetwork. The industrial type has a smaller chip size, which makes it easier to machine and finish, and it has a higher density (usually about 45 to 50 lb./cu. ft.). It is generally available in 1/2-in. and 3/4-in. thicknesses in 49-in. by 97-in. sheet size.

Particle board is an excellent material for many cabinet applications. It is very stable, with little tendency to warp since it has no grain direction. It machines easily and is easy to glue and assemble with conventional and pneumatic fasteners. It is also available with a filled and sanded surface, ready to finish. It is used a great deal for nonexposed cabinet parts such as bottoms, partitions, shelves, wall ends, and countertops.

Hardboard: Hardboard is another sheet product, but instead of being made from wood chips like particle board, the wood is broken down to fibers and then consolidated under heat and pressure in a hot press. The resulting board ranges from tan to dark brown in color and has a very dense, smooth surface. It is water-resistant and can be easily cut, machined, and finished.

Hardboard is available in 4-ft. by 8-ft. sheets in thicknesses ranging from 1/8 in. to 3/8 in., with some special applications available up to 1 in. in thickness. The most common thicknesses are 1/8 in., 3/16 in., and 1/4 in.

Hardboard is available in standard and tempered types. The standard type is sold as it comes from the press and has all the properties previously described. Tempered hardboard has improved hardness and abrasion resistance and is made by subjecting standard hardboard to a treatment of heat, oil, and chemicals. Hardboard is available smooth on one side with a screen-finish back, smooth on both sides, or in a number of embossed or punched patterns. Its primary applications in cabinetwork are cabinet backs, vertical dividers, and drawer bottoms, and some of the embossed or punched patterns are used as door panels.

It also makes an excellent working surface for workbench tops in cabinet shops!

Medium-Density Fiberboard: Medium-density fiberboard is a relatively new product for cabinetmaking. It is similar to particle board in appearance and applications, but it is made from wood fibers in the manner of hardboard. This construction results in a smoother surface finish than particle board, especially on exposed edges. It enjoys great popularity in the furniture industry because its smooth surface allows a woodgrain appearance to be printed on the surface using offset presses, just as a color photograph is printed on paper for a book. It has excellent machining qualities and is often used in core stock for plywood.

Although it is somewhat more expensive than particle board, medium-density fiberboard can be used anywhere that particle board is used in cabinets. It is especially popular for drawer sides for low-priced cabinets and is available in standard drawer-side widths with premachined grooves for the drawer bottom and a wood grain printed on the surface.

Cabinet Liners: A number of products on the market are designed to eliminate the need for finishing cabinet interiors. Most of these are particle board with some type of very hard, smooth surface treatment. The surface coating may be a plastic that is factory-applied in liquid form and then cured by chemical reaction or high temperature, such as Willamette Industries' KORTRON, or it may be a polyester film laminated to the surface, such as Simpson Decra-Guard. Such materials provide a very durable, attractive, and easy-to-clean surface. Often their extra cost is offset by elimination of the finishing operation on the cabinet interior.

HIGH-PRESSURE PLASTIC LAMINATES

Plastic laminates are widely used for countertop coverings. They are very hard, durable sheets that resist heat and stains and are easy to clean. They are popularly known by brand names such as Formica, Texolite, and Nevamar. They are made by impregnating kraft paper with phenolic resins and then laminating these layers in a hot press at very high pressure. Also included in the lamination are a pattern sheet, which may have a printed woodgrain or other pattern, and a transparent cover sheet.

The sheets that are intended for general-purpose use are 1/16-in. thick. Sheets intended for vertical applications such as cabinet faces are 1/32-in. thick. They are usually applied to particle board or plywood using contact cement and are applied after the cabinet is constructed. However, many large production shops laminate sheets of plastic laminate to the particle board or plywood core stock in large presses before cutting component parts.

In residential cabinets, the primary use of plastic laminates is for countertops. Many commercial cabinets, however, have all exposed surfaces and sometimes even the inside surfaces covered with plastic laminate. While this is usually more expensive than wood construction, it results in cabinets that are very durable, resistant to scratching, easy to clean, and which require almost no maintenance.

If laminates are used on components that might be sensitive to warpage, such as cabinet doors, a balance sheet (sheet with no pattern) should be applied to the back surface to seal it from moisture.

ADHESIVES

A number of woodworking adhesives on the market will, if properly used, yield a wood joint stronger than the wood itself. However, they vary in such characteristics as water resistance, heat resistance, chemical resistance, curing time, and gap-filling properties.

For general cabinetwork joinery, a high degree of water resistance is usually not necessary, although cutting-boards should be assembled with a water- and heat-resistant adhesive. Traditionally, woodworking adhesives have been rated in three categories on the basis of moisture resistance: *low moisture resistance*, in which the adhesives do not have to meet any particular standard; *water-resistant*, in which certain prescribed standards must be met; and *waterproof*, a category that has very rigorous standards and requires that the wood fibers break down before the glue line fails.

Curing time is an important consideration in cabinetmaking. If it were necessary to leave each subassembly of a cabinet clamped overnight to cure, the total assembly time would be very long. Therefore, glue with a short curing time is usually desirable except in situations where a complex structure must be assembled in one operation. In such a case, an adhesive with a slow drying time should be selected to allow for getting all the component parts properly clamped and adjusted before the curing begins.

If all joints to be glued are accurately fitted so that there is a high level of contact between mating surfaces, the gap-filling properties of a glue are of little importance. If it becomes necessary to fit parts that are not perfectly mated, however, it is necessary to have an adhesive with good gap-filling properties. Some adhesives are very good at filling small gaps with little loss of strength, while others form a very brittle joint under the same conditions.

Following are descriptions of some of the more popular cabinetmaking adhesives.

Aliphatic Resin Glue: This yellow, ready-to-use glue has a very short clamping time (30 to 45 min. at room temperature), excellent gap-filling properties, good heat resistance, and low moisture resistance. It is probably the most popular glue for assembling cabinets. But its short assembly time makes complex assembly operations difficult.

Polyvinyl Resin: This white, ready-to-use glue is another popular woodworking glue when moisture and heat resistance are not required. It has a fairly short drying time of approximately 1 hr., but a slightly longer assembly time than the aliphatic resin, an advantage in complex assembly situations. It has good gap-filling properties. It is also quite inexpensive.

Liquid Hide Glue: This brown, ready-to-use glue is sometimes used when a very long asembly time is expected. It sets slowly, giving considerable time for final adjustment of component parts. Its curing time in clamps is 10 to 12 hr. It has fair gap-filling properties and low moisture resistance.

Powdered Plastic Resin: This adhesive is sold in powdered form and is mixed with water just before being used. It has very high moisture and heat resistance. It forms a very strong joint when parts are accurately fitted but tends to be somewhat brittle when used with poor-fitting joints. Curing at room temperature takes 12 to 14 hr. But the resin's slow curing time and poor gap-filling properties can be disadvantages, and its strength is subject to following proper mixing procedures. The glue is good for only 2 to 3 hr. after mixing.

Contact Cement: Contact cement is not really a woodworking glue in the same category as the previously listed adhesives and is not recommended for general assembly of wood joints. It is, however, used extensively in cabinetmaking for applying plastic laminate countertops and occasionally for applying thin edge-band material to plywood edges. It is a rubber-based cement which, unlike the previously mentioned adhesives, requires no clamping. Both surfaces to be joined are coated and allowed to dry. They are then brought together and a momentary pressure is applied to complete the bond. The drying process takes place by solvent evaporation, and the drying time required before assembly of the parts will vary from 10 to 20 min. at room temperature for solvent-based cements to 1 hr. or more for water-based cements.

Several other adhesives are occasionally used in cabinetmaking for specific purposes. These include casein glue, which is good for gluing oily tropical woods and is one of the few adhesives that will cure at any temperature above freezing. Another is resorcinol resin, a two-part waterproof adhesive that is mixed before using. It is very expensive and is usually used only when a totally waterproof joint is needed. Epoxies are also expensive and are used for gluing dissimilar materials such as wood to metal, ceramics, or glass.

All the adhesives mentioned except for the contact cement require that the parts being glued be tightly clamped together during the curing period. In practice, this clamping is often accomplished by nailing, stapling, or using other mechanical fasteners to hold the parts while the glue cures.

FASTENERS

Component cabinet parts may be fastened together using nails, staples, screws, bolts, and other fasteners in addition to adhesives. These may be either hand-driven or air-driven.

Nails: While there are many different types of nails for various purposes, only a few types are used for most cabinet assembly. They are shown in Figure 3-26.

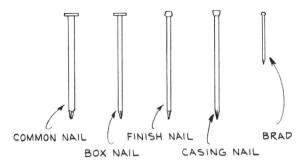

COMMON NAIL   FINISH NAIL   BRAD

BOX NAIL   CASING NAIL

Figure 3-26 Nails used for cabinet assembly

Of the types shown, most work is assembled with box nails, finishing nails, and brads. Nail sizes are designated with an antiquated system that uses penny sizes (abbreviated d) to indicate the length of the nail. A 2-penny (or 2d) nail is 1 in. long. Each additional penny adds 1/4 in. to the length, so a 3d nail is 1 1/4 in. long, a 4d nail is 1 1/2-in. long, and so on to 3 in.

Screws: Wood screws are used when a stronger joint is needed or when it may be necessary to disassemble a joint. They are available with a round head, flat head, or oval head, as shown in Figure 3-27.

The round head is generally used in applications where finished appearance is not important.

Flat-head screws are usually countersunk beneath the surface and covered by a wood plug. Oval-head screws are used in exposed locations and are usually used with a finish washer. They are often bright-plated or finished to match other cabinet hardware.

Screw length is designated in inches and fractions of an inch. Thickness is designated by the gauge size of the shank.

The screw heads may have either a straight slot or a Phillips slot. The Phillips slot is preferred for cabinetwork because it makes the screws much easier to power-drive.

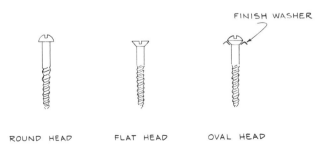

FINISH WASHER

ROUND HEAD   FLAT HEAD   OVAL HEAD

Figure 3-27 Wood screws used for cabinet assembly

Figure 3-28 Pneumatic nailers. (Courtesy of Senco Products, Inc.)

Pneumatic Fasteners: The advent of pneumatic staplers and nailers has greatly reduced the time required for cabinet assembly. Figure 3-28 shows two pneumatic nailers, and Figure 3-29 shows two staplers. Staples are usually used on surfaces that will not be exposed, since they leave a relatively large hole in the wood surface. They do have advantages over nails in that they have less tendency to split the wood and the two legs of the staple are usually designed so that they "clinch" as they are driven into the wood, so they have better holding power than nails.

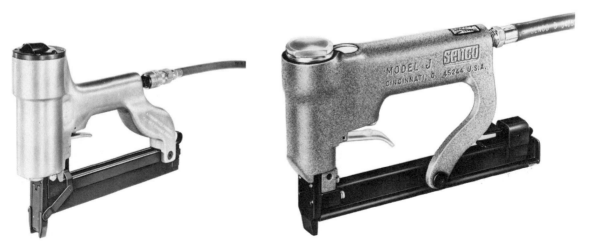

Figure 3-29 Pneumatic staplers. (Courtesy of Senco Products, Inc.)

Figure 3-30 Pneumatic driver for clamp nails for fastening butt joints. (Courtesy of Senco Products, Inc.)

Finish nails are used on exposed surfaces such as face frames and finished ends. The nail gun drives the finish nail slightly below the surface to allow for filling.

There are also special guns that drive special fasteners that are designed to draw butt-jointed wood parts together. Figure 3-30 shows such a gun and its three fasteners.

CABINET HARDWARE

Hinges: Many types and styles of door hinges are available for each of the three basic types of doors described in Chapter 7, namely lip, flush, and overlay. While each of these three basic door types requires a different type of hinge, there are many hinges available for each door type. Hinges may also be classified as surface-mounting hinges, semiconcealed hinges, pivot-pin hinges, and hidden hinges.

Figure 3-31 shows two of the hinges available for lip-type doors. Notice that the semiconcealed type has a step in the door leaf that is designed to fit a 3/8-in. by 3/8-in. rabbet. This hinge is also available in a spring-loaded self-closing type that eliminates the need for door catches.

Figure 3-32 shows two of the hinges available for overlay doors. Notice that the semiconcealed type is very similar to the one used for lip doors, except for the step on the door leaf. These are also available in the self-closing type.

Figure 3-33 shows hinges for flush-fitting doors.

Figure 3-31 Hinges for lip-type doors. (Courtesy of Amerock Corporation)

A relatively new hinge that is often used on lip and overlay doors is the demountable type shown in Figure 3-34. Instead of being attached with screws as conventional hinges are, the demountable type is clamped to the cabinet and to the door. Mounting this hinge requires a special jig for routing the cabinet face frame and door to accept the hinge clamp, but they have many advantages.

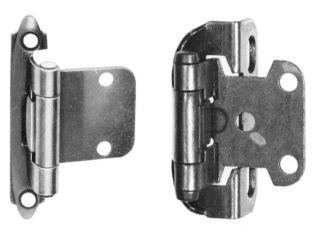

Figure 3-32 Hinges for overlay-type doors. (Courtesy of Amerock Corporation)

Figure 3-33 Hinges for flush-fitting doors

Figure 3-34 Demountable hinge. (Courtesy of Amerock Corporation)

Tightening a single screw secures the hinge to the door, and tightening another screw secures the hinge to the cabinet face. The door is then fully adjustable in any direction merely be loosening one or both screws. This allows doors that are slightly warped to hang properly. If the house settles after the cabinets have been set, the doors can be easily readjusted. It also makes it very easy to install cabinets without the doors attached and then install them on the job site. These hinges are also available in single demountable form, in which the cabinet leaf attaches with screws in the conventional manner and the other leaf clamps to the door. This allows the doors to be adjusted side to side and up and down but not in or out from the face of the cabinet.

Pulls: Drawer and door pulls are available in an almost unlimited number of styles and types. They are usually selected to match the hinge if the hinge is exposed. Some of them are very ornate, but many of these tend to catch dirt and also the clothing of anyone leaning against the cabinets (Figure 3-35).

Door Catches: Door catches are available in magnetic or friction types, but they are not needed when self-closing hinges are used. A touch latch is a special latch that releases the door and springs it open when pressure is applied to the outside of the door. This eliminates the need for a door pull. Touch latches are

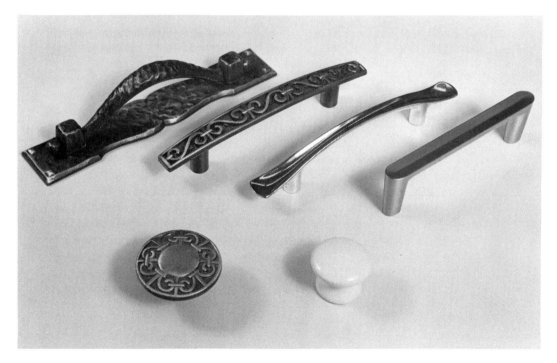

Figure 3-35 Pulls for doors and drawers

Figure 3-36 Set of plastic drawer guides

popular on flush-fitting doors where a clean appearance with no exposed hardware is desired.

Drawer Guides: Drawer-guide systems are described in Chapter 8. The hardware used for the shop-built wood center guide usually consists of a set of plastic tabs, as shown in Figure 3-36. These tabs cover all of the sliding surfaces to reduce friction and to guide the drawer.

Center under-drawer roller guides are also available. These are shown in Figure 3-37. They usually have a 25- to 35-lb. load capacity.

Side roller guides are usually the most desirable (Figure 3-38). They are usually rated at 50 lb. to 75 lb. load capacity and, when properly adjusted, allow the drawer to be moved in or out with very little effort. Most of these require 1/2 in. on either side of the drawer, so in effect they consume 1 in. of available drawer width. These are also available in a full-extension type that allows the drawer to be opened to its full depth.

Side roller guides vary greatly in price, depending on load capacity, smoothness, and other features. They are generally available in 2-in. increments in length.

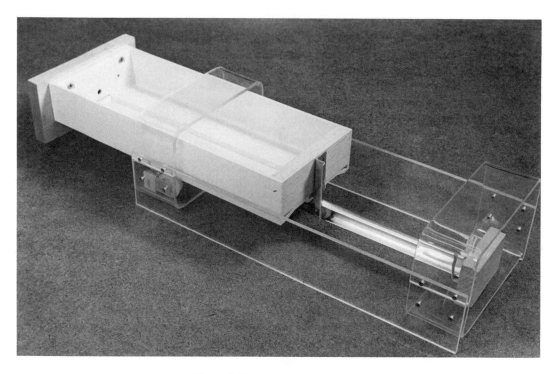

Figure 3-37 Under-drawer roller-guide system

Figure 3-38 Side roller guides

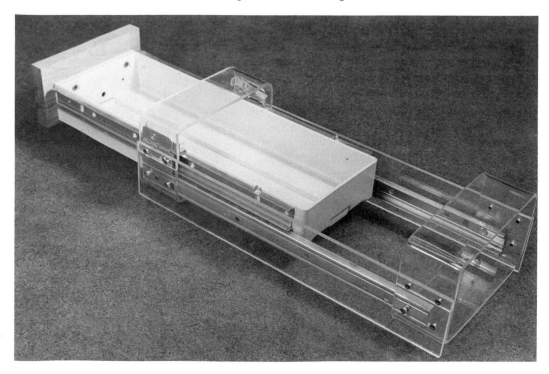

Adjustable Shelf Hardware: Adjustable shelves are usually mounted in cabinets with either of two types of hardware. An adjustable shelf standard, such as the one shown in Figure 3-39, may be used along with matching clips. These give incremental 1/2-in. adjustments in height. These standards must be cut in sets of four so that the numbers match on each piece.

The second method of mounting adjustable shelves requires drilling two vertical rows of 1/4-in.-diameter holes in the wall of the cabinet at either end of the shelf (Figure 3-40). These holes are usually drilled on 1-in. centers. The shelf is then supported by inserting a shelf bracket in each of the four holes at the desired height.

Specialty Hardware: There are many other specialty cabinet hardware items that can make cabinets more attractive, more functional, and easier to use. The cabinetmaker should become familiar with catalogs from some of the manufacturers of the hardware. A listing of a few of these hardware items would include pull-out towel racks, false-drawer-front trays, Lazy Susan hardware, swing-up mixer shelves, under-cabinet cookbook shelves, tambour-door guides, sugar and flour dispensers, among many others.

Figure 3-39 Adjustable shelf standard and clip

Figure 3-40 Adjustable shelf support

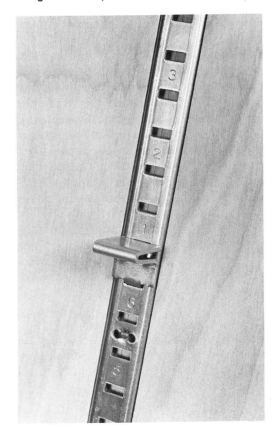

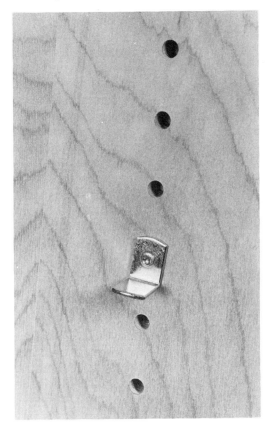

ABRASIVES

Abrasives are used to sand cabinets in preparation for finish and for sanding between coats of finish. In addition, many shops use abrasive planers for sizing wood parts. There are four types of abrasives used on abrasive paper for woodworking: flint, garnet, aluminum oxide, and silicon carbide. These abrasives are bonded to either a paper or a cloth backing, depending on the intended use of the product.

Flint is the least expensive and the least desirable. It is a relatively soft mineral, and as it wears down, it fractures with fairly dull edges. This makes it cut slowly and wear out fast.

Garnet is a natural stone, reddish brown in color. It is much harder and sharper than flint, and as it is worn down, it fractures with sharp edges that form new cutting surfaces. It is used extensively in woodworking, especially for hand sanding.

Aluminum oxide is a by-product of the aluminum manufacturing industry and is a very hard, sharp abrasive. It stands up well to the heat and loads generated in power sanding and is the abrasive used on almost all sanding belts.

Silicon carbide is slightly softer than aluminum oxide, but it fractures with very sharp edges and is available in very fine grits. It is often mounted on waterproof paper and used in wet-sanding operations. In woodworking it is used primarily for sanding between coats of finish and for some finish sanding on raw wood.

The paper backing for abrasives is available in four weights, designated by the letters A (light) through D (heavy). The grit size is designated by the finest wire-mesh screen through which it will pass. A 60-grit abrasive will just pass through a screen with 60 openings per linear inch, a 240-grit will pass through a screen with 240 openings per linear inch, and so on. Abrasive sheets are further classified as open-coat or closed-coat. Open-coat sheets have less abrasive grit on the sheet. The space between grits is used to carry away the wood fibers removed in the sanding operation. An open-coat abrasive has less tendency to fill up than does a closed-coat abrasive, especially when sanding softwoods. A closed-coat sheet is fully covered with abrasive grit. It has more cutting edges, so it will cut faster and smoother, especially in hardwoods.

Cloth backings are much more suitable than paper backings for machine-sanding operations. Cloth backings are available in X (heavy) and J (light) weights.

SUMMARY

This chapter covered most of the materials used in cabinetmaking. Some of the materials described are used only occasionally, while others are used in almost every set of cabinets. Listed here are the basic cabinet components and the materials from which they are most often made:

Cabinet Component	*Typical Material*
Finished ends and finished backs	3/4-in. birch plywood or 3/4-in. red oak plywood
Face frames	solid red oak, birch, or alder
Partitions, bottoms, shelves	3/4-in. industrial particle board, or special cabinet liners
Cabinet backs, drawer bottoms	1/4-in. fir plywood, hardboard, or 1/4-in. hardwood plywood
Drawer sides and backs	1/2-in. hardwood, softwood, medium-density fiberboard, or unidirectional plywood
Doors and drawer fronts	3/4-in. hardwood or hardwood plywood to match finished ends and face frames
Countertop	3/4-in. industrial particle board covered with plastic laminate

Chapter 4

Cabinet Types and Construction Details

By far the most popular types of cabinets found in the typical kitchen are base cabinets and wall cabinets. In this chapter we examine the most common features and construction details of these two types of cabinets.

BASE CABINETS

Base cabinets for kitchen use are usually 36 in. high and 24 in. deep. They consist of two basic parts, the cabinet body and the face frame. The body consists of the cabinet ends, bottom, back, and any partitions or shelves. (The top is added after the cabinets are installed.) The cabinet ends are either finished ends or wall ends, depending on whether they show in the finished product. Finished ends are usually cut from a hardwood plywood to match the rest of the cabinet and are often cut so that they extend slightly beyond the cabinet back so that they may be fitted to a slightly irregular wall. This extension is referred to as a "scribe," as it allows the contour of the wall to be marked or scribed on the cabinet end so that it may be cut or planed to fit the wall. The finished end also has a notch cut from the lower front corner to form the toe space. A nailing strip is placed along the back of the cabinet at the top for installation purposes (Figure 4-1).

Most of the joints on the base cabinets are butt joints assembled with glue and nails or staples. More complex joints are usually not required because base cabinets sit on the floor and the stresses are distributed over a large area.

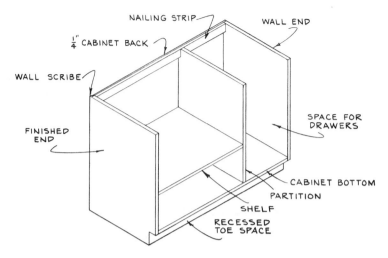

Figure 4-1 Base cabinet shown without face frame

However, if heavy usage is anticipated, it is advisable to use dado and rabbet joints for joining the components. The cabinet back is always rabbeted into finished ends.

Partitions are used to divide various areas within a large cabinet and to support shelves. Partitions are usually used to separate a bank of drawers from the rest of a cabinet, as shown in Figure 4-1. Shelves in base cabinets are quite often fixed at a standard height, usually 11 in. from the bottom of the cabinet. However, space utilization is enhanced by making the shelves adjustable.

Roll-out trays (Figure 2-6) are sometimes used in place of shelves to provide easy access to items in the cabinet. These are similar to drawers in construction and will be discussed in Chapter 8.

The face frame is a very important part of the cabinet. It defines the drawer and door openings and is the mounting surface for door hinges and for some types of drawer guides. It is visible on many types of cabinets and is usually made from a hardwood matching the rest of the cabinet.

If one end of the cabinet is to fit against a wall, the face frame is made slightly longer than the cabinet so that it may be scribed to fit the contour of the wall (Figure 4-2).

The vertical face-frame members on the extreme left and right of the frame are called stiles, and the horizontal pieces are called rails. Vertical members that run between the rails are called mullions (Figure 4-3).

These face-frame members are usually joined in one of three methods, depending on the equipment available in the shop. The strongest method is a mortise-and-tenon joint. This method does require a mortiser and preferably a tenoner as well (Figure 4-4).

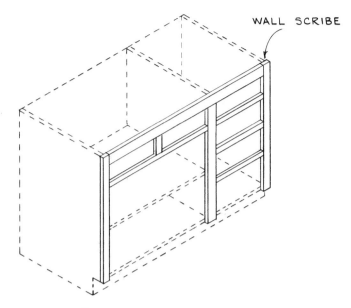

Figure 4-2 Base cabinet with face frame

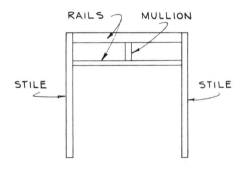

Figure 4-3 Face-frame components

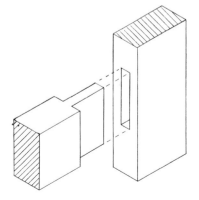

Figure 4-4 Mortise and tenon

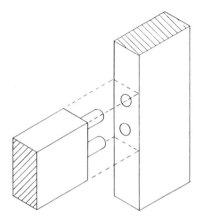

Figure 4-5 Butt joint with dowels

Another joining method often used in the smaller shop is butt joints with dowels (Figure 4-5). The equipment required ranges from simple hand doweling jigs to multispindle boring machines.

A third method of joining face-frame members is to butt the pieces together and drive screws through the joint (Figure 4-6). This requires semiautomated equipment to clamp the frame members together, drill the holes at the proper angles, and install the screws.

Of the three methods, doweling probably requires the least equipment investment. It is important that face-frame members be securely joined. The constant opening and closing of doors, especially those with self-closing hinges, places a considerable load on the joint. The resulting movement between these parts will eventually cause the finish film to crack at the joint if the parts are not properly joined.

Another joining system that can be used for face frames is gaining popularity. This system was developed in Europe and consists of thin elliptical disks glued into elliptical slots cut in the edges of adjoining face-frame members. A special portable power tool is required for machining the slots.

The face frame is glued and assembled as a unit before being attached to the cabinet body.

There are a few other face-frame details worth mentioning at this point. Notice that in all the face-frame illustrations, there are no horizontal bottom rails. This eliminates the necessity of lifting objects over a rail when removing them from the bottom shelf, it makes the bottom shelf easier to clean, and it eliminates one extra step in construction. The front edge of the cabinet bottom

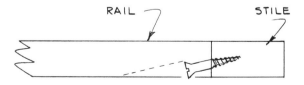

Figure 4-6 Butt joint with screws

Figure 4-7 There is no mullion between the pair of doors on the right side of this cabinet.

is merely covered with an edge banding strip. The doors extend to the bottom of the face-frame rails and thus cover the front edge of the bottom.

It is not necessary to have a mullion between a pair of doors if the doors are fairly narrow (approximately 18 in. wide or narrower). Thus, it is possible to have an opening up to 36 in. wide without a face-frame member to obstruct access to the cabinet (Figure 4-7).

The sizes of face-frame parts will vary somewhat, depending on the type of doors and drawer fronts used (see Chapters 7 and 8), but in general they should not be any wider than necessary. Any unnecessary width of face-frame members encroaches on drawer space and access to cabinet shelf space. The following dimensions are adequate for face-frame members when lip doors and drawers are used. Other types of doors may require more room for mounting hinges. Stiles and mullions are usually 2 in. wide. (Stiles on finished ends are sometimes 1 1/2 in. wide because less of their surface is covered by doors.) Top rails are usually 2 1/2 in. wide to allow room for a pull board. Rails between drawers are usually 1 in. wide (Figure 4-8).

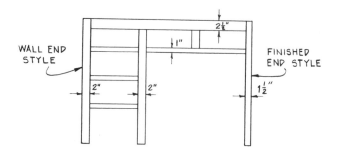

Figure 4-8 Typical face-frame-component sizes

The face frame for a sink cabinet is made as though there were going to be a drawer and doors under the sink. A false drawer front is attached in the drawer opening, or false-front trays, as shown in Figure 4-9, may be installed. Cabinets for surface cooking units (countertop ranges) are similar to the sink cabinet in construction.

A built-in oven requires a special cabinet that extends from the floor to the top of the wall cabinets, with an opening for the oven unit. This cabinet may have doors and a drawer below the oven unit and doors above it. It is usually 25 to 25 1/2 in. deep so that adjacent countertops will not extend beyond the front of this cabinet (Figure 4-10).

Figure 4-9 False-front trays used on a sink cabinet. (Courtesy of Amerock Corporation)

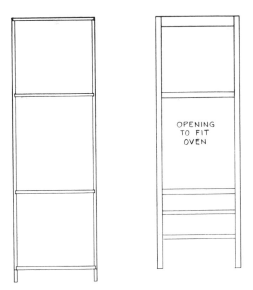

OPENING
TO FIT
OVEN

Figure 4-10 Typical oven cabinet
and face frame

Built-in oven units vary in size, so specifications must be obtained from the manufacturer before the cabinet is designed. If the oven cabinet is floor-to-ceiling, the base must be left loose so that the cabinet can be set in place, lifted, and have the base slipped underneath.

WALL CABINETS

Wall cabinets are usually 12 in. deep and 30 to 36 in. high. Like the base cabinets, they also consist of a body and a face frame. However, the stress loadings on the joints are higher for a cabinet hanging on the wall than they are for one sitting on the floor. Therefore, the structural parts are almost always jointed with rabbet or dado joints.

The wall-cabinet face frame is very similar to that of the base cabinet except that the top rail may be somewhat wider, especially if the cabinets extend to the ceiling. As on the base cabinet, the face frame extends 1/2 in. beyond the end of the cabinet on wall ends so that it may be fitted tightly to the wall (Figure 4-11).

The wall cabinet body is somewhat more complex than that of the base cabinet. Figure 4-12 shows the joinery involved in making the body for a wall cabinet with a finished left end, a wall end on the right, and a partition in the center.

A nailing strip is also included in the wall cabinet for attaching the cabinet to the wall.

Wall cabinets above a range are designed to house an exhaust hood that may be 30 in. or 36 in. wide. The joinery for this cabinet is shown in Figure

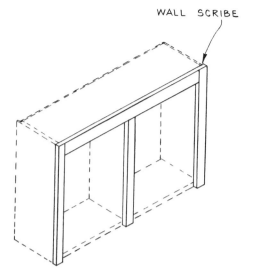

WALL SCRIBE

Figure 4-11 Wall-cabinet face frame

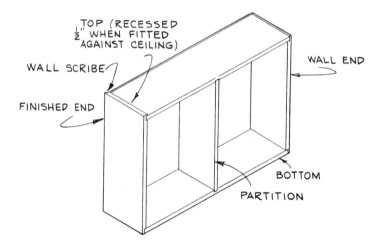

TOP (RECESSED ½" WHEN FITTED AGAINST CEILING)

WALL SCRIBE

WALL END

FINISHED END

BOTTOM

PARTITION

Figure 4-12 Wall-cabinet joinery

4-13. Note that the partitions on either side of the exhaust hood are exposed below the hood and must be machined as finished ends. The center section of this cabinet has the bottom set about 12 in. higher than the bottom of the remainder of the cabinet to accommodate the exhaust hood.

The space left for a refrigerator is usually 36 in. wide by 72 in. high. A special cabinet 36 in. wide and 12 to 18 in. high may be built to go over the

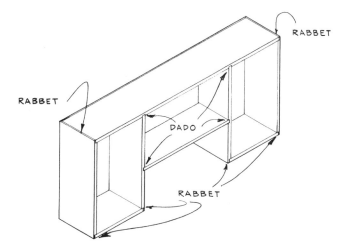

Figure 4-13 Wall cabinet to accommodate range exhaust hood

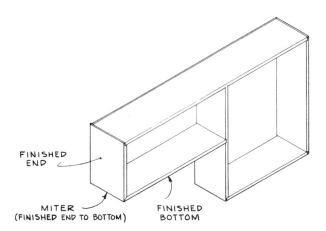

Figure 4-14 Refrigerator-
cabinet construction

refrigerator, or a larger cabinet may be designed to fit beside and above the refrigerator (Figure 4-14).

The bottom surface of a cabinet directly above the refrigerator is somewhat visible and is usually made from the same material as finished ends. It would, in that case, be mitered to the finished end as in Figure 4-14.

Wall cabinets are usually fitted with adjustable shelves. These shelves are supported by clips that attach to a metal shelf standard as shown in Figure 4-15, or they may be supported by clips that are inserted into 1/4-in.-diameter holes drilled in the cabinet walls or partitions as shown in Figure 4-16.

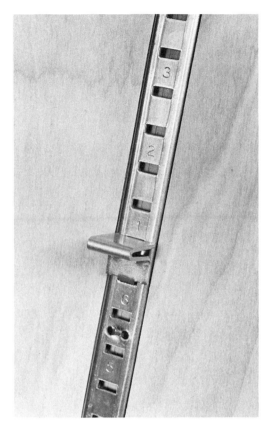

Figure 4-15 Adjustable shelf standard and clip

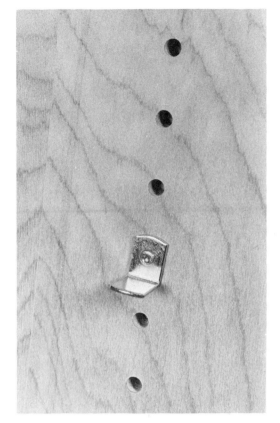

Figure 4-16 Adjustable shelf support

SPECIAL CABINETS

A built-in dishwasher requires no special cabinet. It only requires an opening between base cabinets (usually 24 1/2 in.). The countertop extends over the top of the dishwasher. If the dishwasher is located at the end of a base cabinet and would have an exposed end, a special dishwasher end is made that is very similar to a finished end on a cabinet (Figure 4-17). The dishwasher end supports the countertop and is nailed to the floor at its base.

Corner cabinets present a special problem in space utilization, and there are no easy answers. Figure 4-18 shows three types of corner cabinets.

The L-shaped cabinet shown in Figure 4-18a is actually two cabinets, one of which is placed in the corner and the other then merely butted against it to form the corner. This is the most common and least expensive method because standard cabinet construction is used. It is difficult, however, to reach and

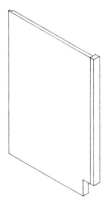

Figure 4-17 Dishwasher end

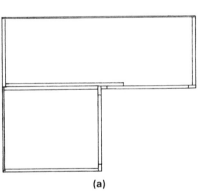

(a)

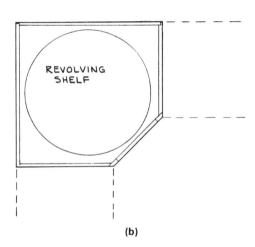

(b)

(c)

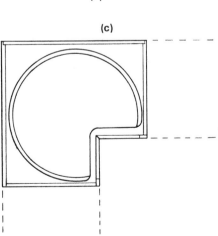

Figure 4-18 Three types of corner cabinets

remove items stored in the corner area, so this storage must be considered only for seldom-used items. This type is acceptable when cabinet space is plentiful.

If this type of cabinet extends into the room to form an eating bar, a door may be placed on the back of the cabinet to provide access to the corner, thus solving the problem.

For kitchens with limited cabinet space, it is usually worth the expense to use corner cabinets such as the ones shown in Figure 4-18b and c. Corner cabinet B is more difficult to construct than A because of the angles involved and does not utilize standard cabinet sheet materials as efficiently. It does, however, provide somewhat easier access to items stored in the corner and can utilize revolving Lazy Susan shelves. It does encroach slightly on room floor space, and it makes reaching the top shelves of the wall cabinet above more difficult.

The Lazy Susan cabinet shown in Figure 4-18c provides easy access to items stored in the corner, but it requires extra time and hardware in its construction. Some such cabinets are built with the door attached directly to the Lazy Susan shelves so that it revolves with the shelves. However, it is difficult, if not impossible, to make this door match the rest of the cabinet doors. Others utilize a hinged L-shaped door. Special hardware must be used so that the revolving shelf unit stops in the proper location for the door to close.

Figure 4-19 shows construction details of the corner cabinet shown in Figure 4-18a. Construction is similar to any other base cabinet except for the face frame.

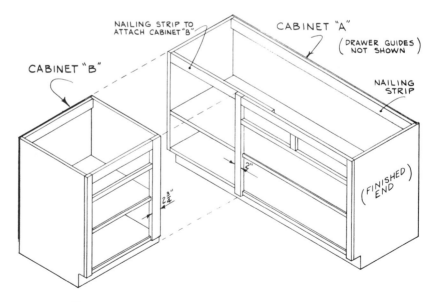

Figure 4-19 Typical method of joining corner base cabinets

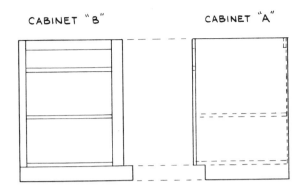

Figure 4-20 Corner cabinet construction. The toe kick board on cabinet "B" is extended to fit the toe space of cabinet "A."

Notice that the face frame on cabinet A stops where it will meet cabinet B. The left stile on cabinet A is 2 in. wide, as usual. The right stile on cabinet B is 2 3/4 in. wide because it extends past the end of the face frame on cabinet A.

It is also necessary to extend the toe kick board on cabinet B to meet the one on cabinet A (Figure 4-20).

BATH CABINETS

Bath vanity cabinets are similar in construction to kitchen base cabinets, with a few minor exceptions. They are usually only 32 in. high, rather than 36 in. They are usually 20 to 22 in. deep, rather than 24 in. If a one-piece cast countertop lavatory is to be used, its dimensions must be obtained and the cabinet built to fit.

The base cabinet will usually have doors under the lavatory area and a bank of drawers on one side if space permits.

Chapter 5

Developing Shop Drawings from Blueprints

BUILDING PLANS

The building drawings prepared by the architect show the general type and location of cabinets to be included in the building. This information is found on the floor plan and, in more detail, on the room elevation plans. A typical room elevation drawing is shown in Figure 5-1.

These drawings provide the basis for more detailed shop drawings. The architect's drawings generally show the following: cabinet sizes, number and location of drawers and doors, side on which doors are hinged, and location of sinks and other major appliances.

From the elevation drawing shown in Figure 5-1, we can obtain the following information regarding the base cabinet:

1. The cabinet is 36 in. high.
2. The cabinet is 60 in. long.
3. It has a sink in the center section.
4. It has a bank of four drawers in the right-hand section. (Drawers are indicated by a rectangle with a diagonal slash.)
5. There is a drawer and a door in the left-hand section. The door hinges on the left-hand side. (Doors are indicated by a rectangle with an arrowhead. The point indicates the hinge side.)
6. There is a pair of doors under the sink.

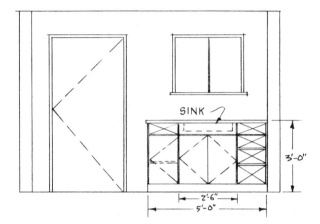

SINK

3'-0"

2'-6"

5'-0"

Figure 5-1 Typical room elevation drawing

These architectural drawings are usually accompanied by a specification book. The section on wood and plastics and the section on finishes will usually include the following information: type of wood cabinets are to be made of, type of door and drawer construction (flush doors, raised panel doors, etc.), type of hardware to be used, type of finish to be used, and type of countertop material to be used.

The specifications for a typical set of cabinets might read as follows:

All exposed cabinet ends and finished backs to be 3/4 in. red oak plywood, rotary cut. All doors to be raised-panel red oak; drawer fronts to be solid red oak; face frames to be clear red oak; cabinet bottoms, shelves, partitions, and unfinished ends to be 3/4-in. industrial-grade particle board with all exposed edges banded with 3/8-in. red oak. Shelves in wall-hung cabinets to be adjustable, using KV 255 shelf standard, hinges to be Amerock 7929AE, and pulls to be Amerock 177A. Drawer sides to be 1/2-in. red alder, drawer bottoms to be 1/4-in. A-D fir plywood.

SHOP DRAWINGS

It might seem that with all this information on hand, cabinet construction could commence at once. Such is not the case. A detailed set of shop drawings must be prepared and presented to the architect or to the customer for approval. The person preparing the shop drawings usually takes measurements on the job site of the finished rooms where the cabinets are to be located. This is very important, because the dimensions specified by the architect on the blueprints were determined before actual construction of the building started. These dimensions may have changed significantly by the time the building is ready for cabinets.

In addition to accurate overall cabinet dimensions, the shop drawings must include accurate dimensions of each door and drawer opening and of all face-

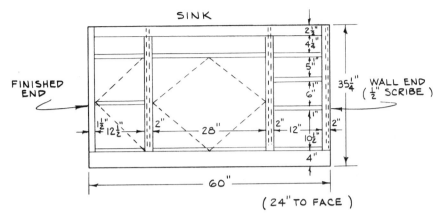

Figure 5-2 Typical shop drawing of the cabinet shown in Figure 5-1

frame parts. Cabinet ends must be designated as finished ends (exposed) or wall ends. The type of door and drawer must be indicated, and any special features must be noted.

Most shops develop a general routine for building cabinets over a period of time, and they usually find that it is not necessary to include all the routine details in every set of shop drawings. A somewhat simplified system of preparing shop drawings evolves. For example, if the same type of drawer guide system is always used, it is not necessary to draw this in detail on each set of drawings. This saves time in preparing the shop drawings.

These shop drawings usually show the face of the cabinet without drawers or doors. This is often the only view necessary.

Figure 5-2 shows a shop drawing of the cabinet shown in Figure 5-1. Notice that the drawing concentrates on the face-frame detail. The construction of the cabinet body is fairly standard, with most of the components being assembled with butt joints as described in Chapter 4. The features of the cabinet body that are shown are the shelf, the partitions, and the right end of the cabinet body. (The face frame extends 1/2 in. past the right end of the cabinet body to fit against the wall.)

ON-SITE MEASUREMENTS

Before the shop drawings can be prepared, accurate measurements must be taken of the location where the cabinets are to be installed. If the building plans show an elevation view of the cabinets, this may be traced and the actual dimensions, as determined by measurement, noted on this tracing. These dimensions will then be used to prepare the actual drawing. If a measurement between two walls is being taken, it should be taken at several points to check for variations. Figure 5-3 shows typical measurements taken for base cabinets.

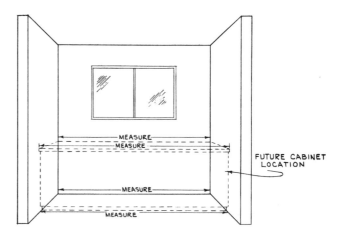

Figure 5-3 Points to measure when cabinets are to fit between walls

PREPARING SHOP DRAWINGS

Shop cabinet drawings are not especially difficult to prepare as they consist mostly of simple rectangular shapes. However, they should be neatly and accurately done to minimize the chance of error in the actual cabinet construction.

The equipment required for preparing shop cabinet drawings includes a drawing board or table, a T square, an architect's scale (usually 1 in. = 1 ft.), triangles, mechanical lead holder or pencil, lead pointer, and paper. This equipment is shown in Figures 5-4 through 5-8.

If the drawing is to be reproduced as a blueprint for shop use, it must be prepared on a semitransparent paper such as drafting vellum or on one of the mylar films available for this purpose. The drawing may be done directly on the vellum or on an inexpensive paper and then traced on the vellum. If the drawing is made directly on the vellum, it must be done very carefully. This usually requires preparing the drawing with light lines, erasing unwanted lines, and darkening the finished lines. I prefer to rough out the drawing quickly on inexpensive paper, then tape the vellum over this paper and trace the finished drawing. This usually eliminates any erasures and has proved to be just as fast in spite of the extra operation. This is the method that will be described here.

Before beginning the actual drawing, some thought should be given to the layout on the paper. The cabinets are usually drawn in the relative position that they will occupy in the room. If all of the cabinets forming a U-shaped kitchen are to be drawn on one sheet of paper, a logical place to start would be at one end of the U, as shown in Figure 5-9. The layout of the drawing would be as shown in Figure 5-10.

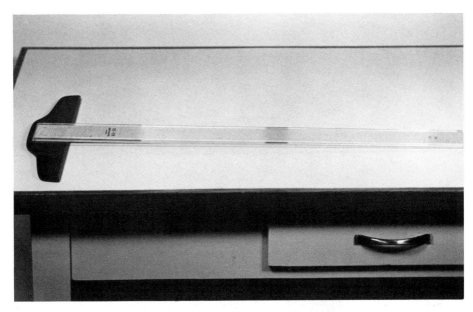

Figure 5-4 Drawing board and T square

Figure 5-5 Architect's scale

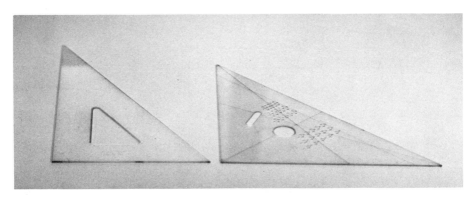

Figure 5-6 45° and 30°-60° triangles

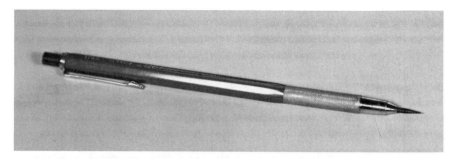

Figure 5-7 Lead holder

Figure 5-8 Lead pointer

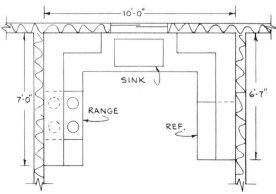

Figure 5-9 Layout of a U-shaped kitchen

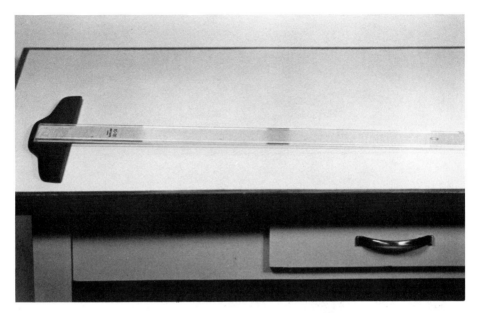

Figure 5-4 Drawing board and T square

Figure 5-5 Architect's scale

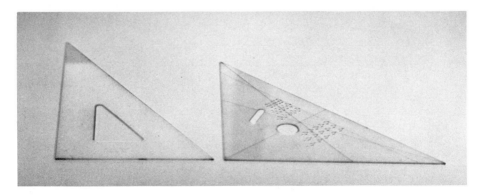

Figure 5-6 45° and 30°-60° triangles

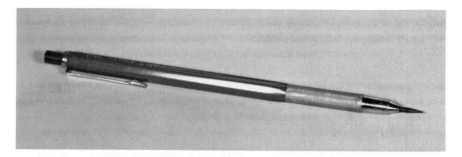

Figure 5-7 Lead holder

Figure 5-8 Lead pointer

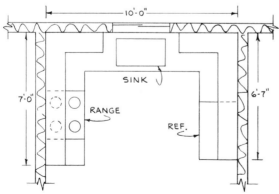

Figure 5-9 Layout of a U-shaped kitchen

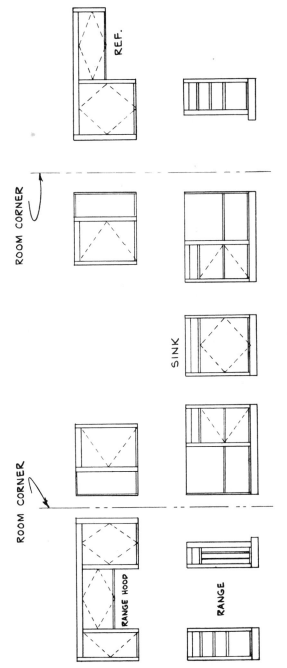

Figure 5-10 Shop drawing layout for U-shaped kitchen shown in Figure 5-9

71

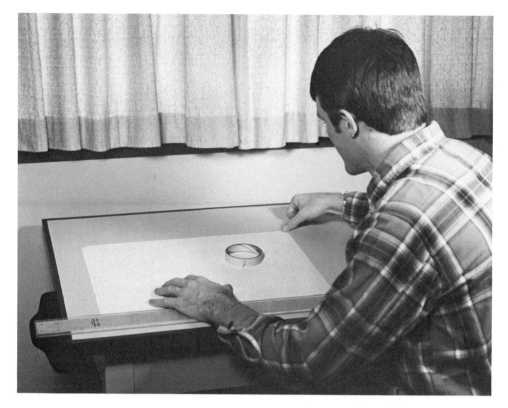

Figure 5-11 Taping paper to the drawing board

Once the layout has been determined, the drawing may be started. The paper for the rough drawing is taped to the drawing board so that the bottom edge is parallel with the bottom edge of the board (Figure 5-11). The T square is used as a guide for all horizontal lines. The head of the T square slides along the left-hand edge of the board so that the blade of the square is always perpendicular to the edge (Figure 5-12). The pencil lead is pointed and the point slightly rounded on a piece of scrap paper (Figure 5-13). The pencil is drawn (not pushed) along the blade of the square. On long lines, the pencil should be rotated slightly as it is being drawn to prevent the line from becoming thicker as the point wears flat. If a rough drawing is being prepared for later tracing, a soft lead should be used to produce dark lines that can be easily seen through the tracing vellum.

To start the rough drawing, a horizontal line is drawn near the bottom of the paper. This line is drawn all the way across the paper and represents the bottom of the base cabinets. Using the 1-in. scale, another horizontal line is drawn 35 1/4 in. above the first (measured on the 1 in. = 1 ft. scale). This represents the top of the base cabinets (minus the countertop).

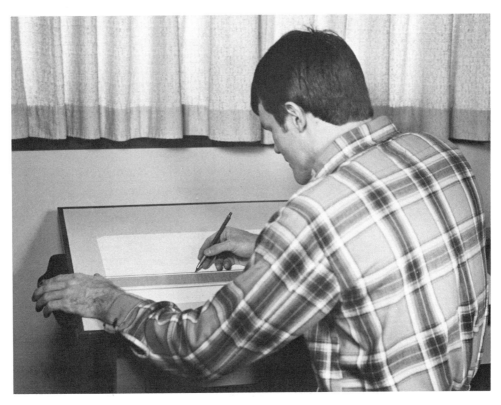

Figure 5-12 Using the T square

Figure 5-13 Using the pencil pointer

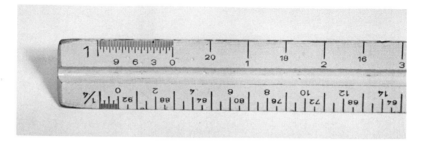

Figure 5-14 Architect's scale showing 1 in. = 1 ft. scale

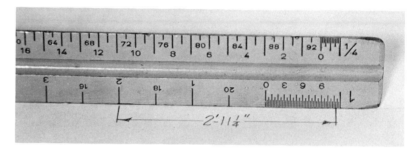

Figure 5-15 Measuring 35 1/4 in. (2 ft. 11 1/4 in.) on the 1-in. scale

The architect's scale shows scale dimensions in feet and inches. The 1-ft. segment at the extreme left or right of the scale is divided into inches and fractions of an inch (Figure 5-14). To measure 35 1/4 in., measure 2 ft. 11 1/4 in. (Figure 5-15). To locate the bottom of the wall cabinets, another horizontal line is drawn 16 3/4 in. above the base cabinets, and a fourth horizontal line is drawn 30 in. above this line to represent the top of the wall cabinets (assuming that the wall cabinets are 30 in. high). The paper will now look something like the one shown in Figure 5-16.

Figure 5-16 Layout of horizontal lines for base and wall cabinets

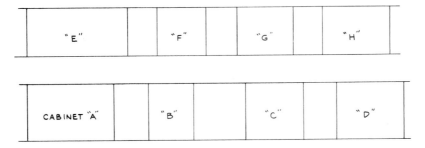

Figure 5-17 Vertical lines representing left and right side of each cabinet

Now lay out the location of all the base and wall cabinets, leaving enough space between each one for dimensions and any necessary notations. Vertical lines are then drawn to represent the left and right sides of each cabinet (Figure 5-17).

We now focus on a single cabinet for completing the working drawings; each cabinet is drawn in a similar manner. From the bottom line on the base cabinet, measure up 4 in. and draw a horizontal line the length of the cabinet. This represents the toe space at the bottom of the cabinet (Figure 5-18).

The face-frame stiles are drawn next. These are usually 1 1/2 in. wide on a finished end or 2 in. wide on a wall end (Figure 5-19).

The top face-frame rail is drawn next. This is usually 2 1/2 in. wide (Figure 5-20).

Next, the mullion is drawn (Figure 5-21) and then the other rails and mullions (Figure 5-22). The bottom of the cabinet and any shelves and partitions are now drawn (Figure 5-23). If the cabinet has doors, the hinge side must be noted with the arrow, as shown in Figure 5-1 (Figure 5-24).

Next, dimension and extension lines must be put on the drawing and all dimensions noted. Dimensioning is critical, so care must be taken to show the

Figure 5-18 Cabinet toe kick space

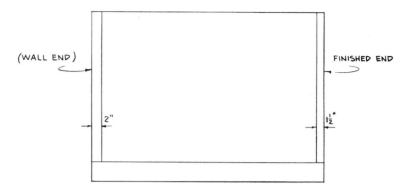

Figure 5-19 Face-frame stiles

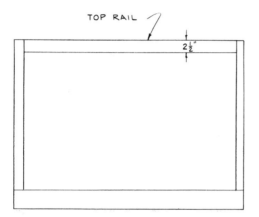

Figure 5-20 Face-frame top rail

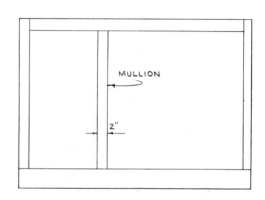

Figure 5-21 Face-frame mullion

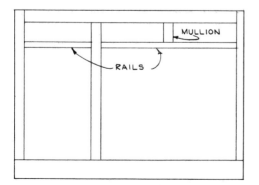

Figure 5-22 Face-frame rails and mullion

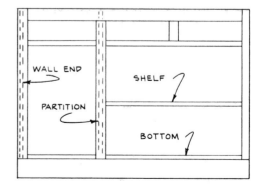

Figure 5-23 Cabinet bottom, shelf, and partition

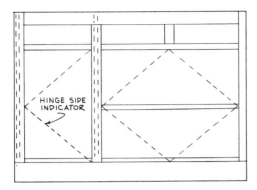

Figure 5-24 Dotted arrows indicating hinge side of the doors

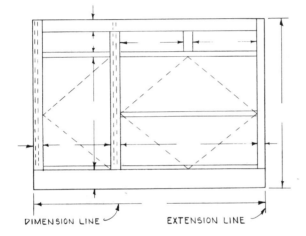

Figure 5-25 Dimension and extension lines

exact point of reference of each dimension. Extension lines are extension of lines on the object showing the location of the dimension (Figure 5-25).

The dimension line has an arrowhead on each end to show the point of reference. On the shop drawings, all dimensions are expressed in inches rather than in feet and inches, as they were on the architectural building plans. On cabinets, there are a number of small measurements that must be expressed in inches and fractions of an inch, so it is much easier for the cabinetmaker if all dimensions are in inches. It would be very easy, for example, to read a plan dimension as 2 ft. 6 in. and then set the saw for a 26-in. cut; having everything listed in inches eliminates the possibility of making this mistake. The dimensions needed on the drawing include: the overall width and height, the width and height of each opening in the face frame, and the width of each face-frame member. These are shown in Figure 5-26.

Finally, any notations about the cabinet or type of construction must be made. When only the front view is shown, as on these drawings, the cabinet depth must be noted. Notations on whether the cabinet ends are finished ends or unfinished (wall) ends must be made (Figure 5-27).

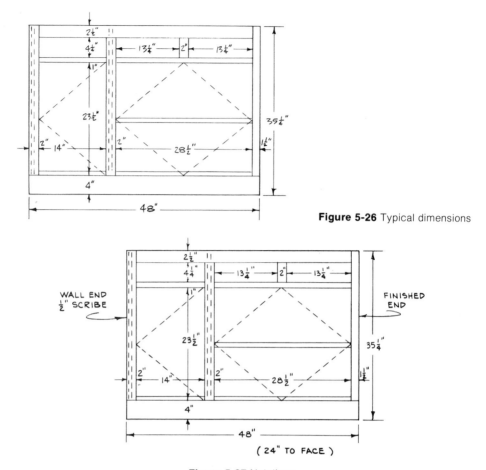

Figure 5-26 Typical dimensions

Figure 5-27 Notations

Other features usually indicated by notations include sink location, pull-board location, adjustable shelves, roll-out trays, type of hinges and hardware, type of material, and anything else that is not standard.

It is very helpful to identify each cabinet of a set by a letter. Later, when the cabinet parts are being cut and machined, each part of cabinet A is marked with an A, each part of cabinet B is marked B, and so on. These parts are then kept in separate stacks for easy identification and assembly.

THE CUTTING LIST

If there is any secret to achieving speed and accuracy and eliminating mistakes in cutting out cabinet parts, it is this: *Make a cutting list*. The cutting list is a list of the parts that are required to make the cabinet and their dimensions. The

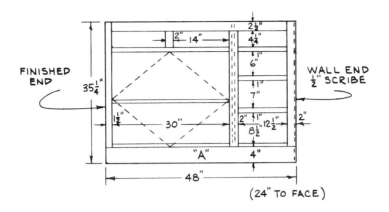

CABINET "A" CUTTING LIST

OAK PLYWOOD :
1	Pc.	$\frac{3}{4}$ X 23$\frac{1}{4}$ X 35$\frac{1}{4}$	FINISHED END
1	Pc.	$\frac{3}{4}$ X 4 X 48	BASE FRONT

PARTICLE BOARD :
1	Pc.	$\frac{3}{4}$ X 22$\frac{3}{4}$ X 46	BOTTOM
1	Pc.	$\frac{3}{4}$ X 22$\frac{3}{4}$ X 31$\frac{3}{8}$	SHELF
1	Pc.	$\frac{3}{4}$ X 22$\frac{3}{4}$ X 31$\frac{1}{4}$	WALL END
1	Pc.	$\frac{3}{4}$ X 22$\frac{3}{4}$ X 30$\frac{1}{2}$	PARTITION

FIR PLYWOOD :
1	Pc.	$\frac{3}{4}$ X 2$\frac{1}{2}$ X 46	NAILING STRIP
1	Pc.	$\frac{1}{4}$ X 31$\frac{1}{4}$ X 47$\frac{1}{4}$	BACK
1	Pc.	$\frac{3}{4}$ X 4 X 46$\frac{3}{8}$	BASE BACK
4	Pc.	$\frac{3}{4}$ X 4 X 19	BASE BLOCKS

SOLID OAK - FACE FRAME :
1	Pc.	$\frac{3}{4}$ X 2$\frac{1}{2}$ X 46$\frac{1}{2}$	TOP RAIL
1	Pc.	$\frac{3}{4}$ X 1$\frac{1}{2}$ X 31$\frac{1}{4}$	STILE
1	Pc.	$\frac{3}{4}$ X 2 X 31$\frac{1}{4}$	STILE
1	Pc.	$\frac{3}{4}$ X 2 X 30$\frac{3}{4}$	MULLION
1	Pc.	$\frac{3}{4}$ X 1 X 32	RAILS
3	Pc.	$\frac{3}{4}$ X 1 X 14$\frac{1}{2}$	RAILS
1	Pc.	$\frac{3}{4}$ X 2 X 6$\frac{1}{2}$	MULLION

Figure 5-28 Cabinet and cutting list

cutting list is usually prepared from the shop drawings by the person who will be cutting out the cabinets. With an accurate cutting list, the person cutting out the cabinets is able to quickly cut all the parts accurately to finished size without having to take time to interpret the drawing while cutting. After the parts have been cut to size, the cabinetmaker then refers to the drawing to determine further machining operations.

Figure 5-28 shows a shop drawing of a base cabinet and a cutting list for it. This is the cutting list for the entire cabinet and face frame. The doors and drawers are usually done on a separate list. These will be discussed in Chapters 7 and 8. The particle-board countertop is also not included. It is installed after the cabinets have been installed and is usually cut to cover more than one individual cabinet.

Notice also that the dimensions are *always* listed in this order: thickness, width, and length. This is very important, especially when cutting plywood. Otherwise, there will be confusion about the grain direction. For example, the first item on the cutting list in Figure 5-28 is a finished end marked 3/4 × 23 1/4 × 35 1/4; it would be cut as shown in Figure 5-29a, with the grain running vertically. (The width direction is always across the grain.) If instead the list read 3/4 × 35 1/4 × 23 1/4, the 35 1/4-in. dimension would be understood to be the width and the part would be cut as shown in Figure 5-29b.

We now look at the cutting list to determine how the size of each part was derived from the drawing.

- 1 pc 3/4 × 23 1/4 × 35 1/4 finished end, oak plywood

The notation at the bottom of the drawing indicates that that cabinet is 24 in. deep (24 in. to face), including the 3/4-in.-thick face frame. Therefore, the end of the cabinet is 23 1/4 in. wide. Base cabinets are usually 36 in. high,

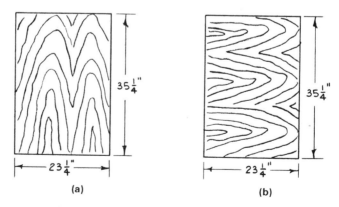

(a)   (b)

Figure 5-29 The sequence of listing width and length determines grain direction

including the countertop. The cabinet without the 3/4-in. countertop would then be 35 1/4 in., so this becomes the length of the end.

• 1 pc 3/4 × 4 × 48 baseboard, oak plywood

The toe space is 4 in. high, so this is the width of the front baseboard; the length is merely the length of the cabinet.

• 1 pc 3/4 × 22 3/4 × 46 bottom, particle board

If you turn back to Figure 4-1, you will notice that the finished end has a 1/2-in. rabbet for the 1/4-in. plywood back (the remaining 1/4 in. is for fitting the cabinet to the wall). Therefore, the cabinet bottom is 1/2 in. narrower (22 3/4 in.) than the finished end (Figure 5-30).

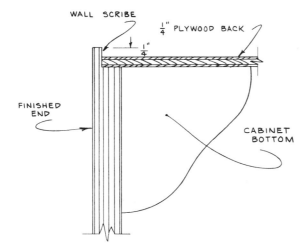

Figure 5-30 A 1/2-in. by 1/2-in. rabbet in a finished end for the cabinet back

The length of the cabinet bottom (46 in.) is obtained by subtracting the thickness of both ends (3/4 in. + 3/4 in. = 1 1/2 in.) plus, in this case, the 1/2-in. scribe on the wall end. In this case, the face frame is 48 in. wide, but the cabinet body is only 47 1/2 in. Therefore, the bottom is 46 in. long.

• 1 pc 3/4 × 22 3/4 × 31 3/8 shelf, particle board

The shelf width is the same as that of the bottom (22 3/4 in.). The length is designated so that the shelf will extend from the finished end to the partition, which is centered behind the center face-frame mullion. Therefore, the length of the shelf would include the cabinet opening (30 in.) plus 3/4 in. on the left side plus 5/8 in. on the right side (2 in. face frame minus 3/4 in. centered par-

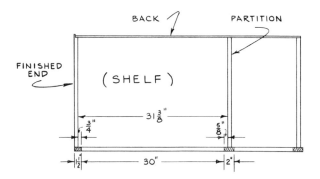

Figure 5-31 Plan view of the cabinet showing how the shelf length was determined

tition = 5/8 in. on each side of the partition) for a total length of 31 3/8 in. (Figure 5-31).

- 1 pc 3/4 × 22 3/4 × 31 1/4 wall end, particle board

The back does not need to be rabbeted into the wall end since it will not show. Therefore, the wall end is also the same width as the bottom (22 3/4 in.). It does not run to the floor but attaches to the bottom, as shown in Figure 5-32, so it is 4 in. shorter (31 1/4 in.) than the finished end.

- 1 pc 3/4 × 22 3/4 × 30 1/2 partition, particle board

Again, the width (22 3/4 in.) is the same as that of the bottom. The partition sits on the bottom, so it is 3/4 in. shorter than the wall end (Figure 5-32).

- 1 pc 3/4 × 2 1/2 × 46 nailing strip, fir plywood

This is the strip shown in Figure 4-1 used to nail the cabinet to the wall. It is usually 2 1/2 in. wide and the same length as the cabinet bottom (46 in.).

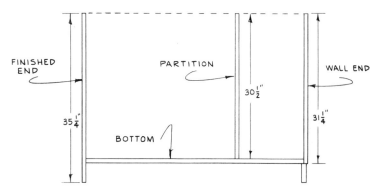

Figure 5-32 Front view of the cabinet body showing how the heights of the wall end and partitions are determined

- 1 pc 1/4 × 31 1/4 × 47 1/4 back, fir plywood

The back of the cabinet extends from the top of the cabinet to the bottom edge of the bottom (31 1/4 in.). The length of the back is equal to the length of the cabinet body (47 1/2 in.) minus the 1/4-in. thickness of the finished end scribe (47 1/4 in. total length) (Figure 5-33).

- 1 pc 3/4 × 4 × 46 3/8 base back, fir plywood

The base on the cabinet would be assembled as shown in Figure 5-34.
The base back is the length of the cabinet bottom plus 3/8 in. This places the end base block under the joint between the cabinet bottom and the wall end.

- 4 pcs 3/4 × 4 × 19 base blocks, fir plywood

These are the blocks shown in Figure 5-34; they merely transfer the weight of the cabinet to the floor.
The face frame is shown in detail on the shop drawings, so its dimensions are easy to obtain from the drawings. The cutting list shown for the face frame in Figure 5-28 assumes that mortise-and-tenon joints are used to join all parts.

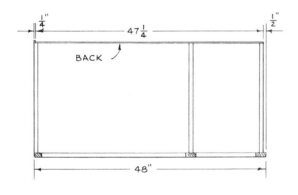

Figure 5-33 Plan view of the cabinet showing how the length of the back is determined

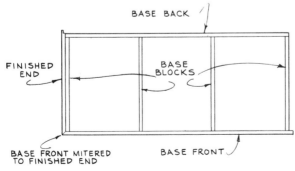

Figure 5-34 Plan view showing construction of the cabinet base

Therefore, 1 in. has been added for a tenon at each joint. For example, the width of the drawer opening is 12 1/2 in., so the rails between the drawers are 14 1/2 in. long to allow for the 1-in. tenon at each end. If butt joints with dowels or screws were used, the parts would be cut to exact lengths.

The importance of this cutting list cannot be overemphasized. It serves several very important purposes. Any errors in the drawing or dimensions are usually caught while making the cutting list rather than after expensive material has been cut. It allows the cabinetmaker to group together any pieces with identical dimensions so that they can all be cut at the same machine setting. This improves accuracy and eliminates setup time. It also prevents duplication of parts. As each part is cut, it is crossed off the list so it will not be recut. This is especially important when the cabinetmaker is cutting out several cabinets at once.

The first time you develop a cutting list from a drawing will probably require a great deal of thought to determine the dimension of each part. However, with a little practice, a pattern soon develops. If the depth and height of the cabinets are standard, then the only variables are the length and internal configurations. Therefore, a number of parts will always be the same size. These dimensions are soon remembered. In fact, many shops cut a great quantity of these standard parts in advance and then only have to cut the non-standard parts for each job. The cutting list for the cabinet shown in Figure 5-28 took less than 5 min. to prepare.

Chapter 6

Machining and Assembling the Face Frame

The face frame is often made and assembled before the cabinet is built because it takes less room to store an assembled face frame than it does an assembled cabinet. In fact, it is best if the face frame, drawers, and doors are all built before the cabinet body is assembled. This allows the face frame, doors, and drawers to be fitted to the cabinet before it is moved from the assembly bench. If these parts are not ready for installation when the cabinet body is assembled, it must be moved to a storage area then brought back for final assembly.

The joinery used to assemble the face-frame parts is important. There are heavy loads involved, especially when self-closing hinges are used for the doors. The most popular joints used for joining face-frame members are the mortise-and-tenon joint, the butt joint with dowels, and the butt joint with screws, as shown in Figures 4-4 through 4-6. The mortise-and-tenon joint is the strongest and is used in most of the examples in this chapter.

For cabinets built for commercial use, and even for some residential cabinets, the architect may specify one of three levels of construction quality as specified by the Architectural Woodwork Institute.* This may determine the type of joint used.

*"Architectural Woodwork Quality Standards and Guide Specifications" (Arlington, Va.: Architectural Woodwork Institute, 1973).

SIZING ROUGH LUMBER

Face-frame parts and other solid wood parts are often cut from rough-sawn hardwood lumber. When this is the case, the lumber must be straightened and planed to a uniform thickness before the face frame or other parts are cut to size. Rough-sawn lumber is often warped, so it is important that the cabinet-maker understand the process for truing up warped lumber.

The first step in truing warped lumber is to joint one face on the jointer (Figure 6-1). It is important that the board not be allowed to rock while being face-jointed. This will cause the jointed surface to have a twist or bow. The board must be held flat as it passes over the knives so that the high spots are planed off and the board will lie flat.

A push block such as the one shown in Figure 6-1 should be used when face-jointing lumber, and a fairly light cut should be taken.

After the board has been jointed on one face, the opposite face is planed parallel with the first, using a thickness planer (Figure 6-2).

Figure 6-1 Face-jointing a warped board. Note the push block used when face-jointing lumber.

Figure 6-2 Using the thickness planer to plane lumber to final thickness

When these two operations have been properly completed, the board will be flat and uniform in thickness. The board may now be planed down to its final desired thickness. If a number of boards are to be planed to the same thickness, they should all be face-jointed first and then all planed to thickness as a group so that the final sizing is done at one machine setting. This ensures that all boards are a uniform thickness, which will facilitate later joining operations.

It should be noted that the thickness planer and the jointer serve different purposes in truing and surfacing rough stock. The thickness planer alone will not straighten twisted or crooked boards. It will merely plane the top surface of a board (on single-head models) parallel to the bottom surface. If a rough, twisted board is planed, the finished result will be a smooth, twisted board! The jointer, on the other hand, will establish a flat surface on one face of the board by planing the high spots flat. However, if the board is then turned over and the second face is planed on the jointer, there is no assurance that it will be parallel to the first face. Therefore, both machines are needed to true warped lumber. If a wide jointer and thickness planer are not available, presurfaced lumber should be purchased.

After the boards have been trued and planed to thickness, the next step is to establish a straight edge on each board. This is also done on the jointer (Figure 6-3).

Figure 6-3 Edge-jointing a board

CUTTING FACE-FRAME PARTS

We are now ready to rip the boards into stock face-frame widths, using the table saw. The drawing and cutting list in Figure 5-28 shows the widths of typical face-frame components to be 2 1/2 in., 2 in., 1 1/2 in., and 1 in., so we should cut sufficient material in each of these widths to make the required number of parts. When ripping boards to width, the widest parts on the list should be cut first, then the next widest, and so forth. The narrow parts can often be cut from the waste material that remains after making the wide cuts. Figure 6-4 shows the face-frame parts being cut to width.

There is one other important consideration in cutting face-frame material. Any edge of a face-frame member that is visible on the finished cabinet should have a planed edge rather than a sawn edge. For example, the left stile on the finished end of the cabinet will show on both edges, so both edges must be planed. The 2 1/2-in. top rail, however, will be covered by the countertop on the top edge, and the bottom edge is hidden by drawers, so it may have sawn edges. The pieces that require planed edges must be cut slightly oversize (1/32 to 1/16 in.) to allow for planing to final width on the jointer (Figure 6-5).

Figure 6-4 Ripping the face-frame material to standard widths. Notice the push stick used for cutting narrow boards on the table saw. (The saw guard has been removed for clarity in showing the operation.)

Figure 6-5 Edge-planing a face-frame part to final width to remove saw marks

The table saw, if used improperly, can be a potentially dangerous machine. The operator should be thoroughly familiar with its operation before attempting to use it. In addition to the general safety rules that apply when operating other machines, the following rules should be observed:

1. The height of the saw blade should be adjusted so that it protrudes only 1/8 to 1/4 in. above the surface of the material being cut.

2. A push stick such as the one shown in Figure 6-4 should be used for pushing narrow boards between the saw blade and the rip fence. Note that the board remaining between the fence and the blade must be pushed past the rear of the blade before being released.

3. One should never attempt to make freehand cuts on the table saw. The slightest twisting will cause the board to bind on the saw blade and be thrown back at the operator. The rip fence must be used when ripping long boards to width, and the sliding miter gauge, as shown in Figure 6-6, must be used when cross-cutting boards to length. Boards to be ripped against the rip fence must have a straight edge against the fence and a flat face to lay on the table to prevent possible binding. The miter gauge and rip fence are not to be used at the same time.

Figure 6-6 Using the table-saw miter gauge for crosscutting

After pieces are cut to standard widths, they are cut to the lengths as listed on the cutting list, using the radial-arm saw (Figure 6-7).

The rough ends should be trimmed and checked for any splits before the finished lengths are cut.

Figure 6-7 Cutting face-frame parts to length on the radial-arm saw

LAYOUT FOR MACHINING

Once the parts are cut to finish sizes, the location of the mortise-and-tenon or other joints must be marked on the parts. Before the layout process begins, each part should be examined to determine the better face to be exposed. The back surface of each board is then marked (Figure 6-8). The reasons for this will become apparent when we begin machining the face frame.

The face-frame members are then set on a bench in the positions that they will occupy on the finished frame (Figure 6-9). The end of each member that is to have a tenon is marked (Figure 6-10). The location of each mortise is also marked.

If dowels are being used rather than mortise-and-tenon joints, the process is similar and the location of the dowel centers is marked.

Figure 6-8 The back side of each face-frame part is marked.

Figure 6-9 Face-frame parts set in position for layout marking

Figure 6-10 All ends to be tenoned are marked.

MACHINING FACE-FRAME JOINTS

The mortise part of the mortise-and-tenon joint is usually machined first because the thickness of the cut is established by the size of the mortising chisel. The tenon thickness can then be adjusted to fit.

The mortises are cut on a hollow chisel mortiser such as the one shown in Figures 6-11 and 6-12. If the tenons are to be 1-in. long, for example, the mortises should be at least 1 1/8 in. deep to allow space for excess glue and wood chips.

The face of each board should be placed against the guide fence on the mortiser. The mark that you made on the back side of the board will be visible on the outside (Figure 6-13). This is very important. If the mortise is not located in the exact center of the board, it will not matter as long as all boards are machined with the face side against the fence. However, if some of the boards are machined with the back side against the fence and the mortise is not centered, the face surfaces of the joint will be offset, as shown in Figure 6-14. The same is true when locating dowel holes. The mortises are now machined at all locations as marked.

If the mortise occurs at the end of a board—as it would at the top of a stile where it accepts the top rail, for example—the mortise should not be machined to full depth all the way to the end of the board, as this would make it easy to split the board. Instead, the mortise and tenon are haunched as shown in Figure 6-15.

The tenons may be machined in a number of ways. Single-end tenon machines, as shown in Figure 6-16, work very well but often are not available in the smaller shop. Tenons may also be easily and accurately machined on a table saw with a good dado set. Figure 6-17 shows a tenon being cut on a table saw.

Figure 6-11 Hollow chisel mortiser

Figure 6-12 Machining the mortise

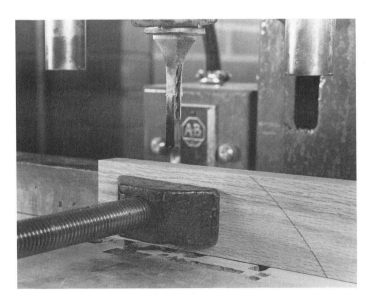

Figure 6-13 Mounting the board in the mortiser with face to fence (mark out)

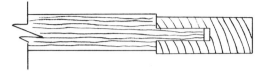

Figure 6-14 Mortise-and-tenon joint not properly centered

Figure 6-15 Haunched mortise and tenon

Figure 6-16 Single-end tenoner

Figure 6-17 Machining a tenon
using a table saw with a dado set

Notice that the miter gauge is used to push the stock through the cutter and the rip fence is used as a guide to ensure that both shoulder cuts are exactly equal. Normally, the rip fence and miter gauge are not used together, but in this case no piece is being cut off that could become trapped between the blade and fence and thrown from the machine. The depth of the dado cut establishes the thickness of the tenon. The tenons on the top rails must then be haunched as shown in Figure 6-18.

Figure 6-19 shows the machined parts of a face frame ready for assembly.

If a pull board (breadboard) is specified for a cabinet, its opening should be cut in the top face-frame rail before the face frame is assembled. If the pull board is 3/4 in. thick, the face-frame opening is 13/16 in. wide. The top of the opening is usually 1 in. from the top of the rail.

Figure 6-18 Haunching tenons
on the top rail

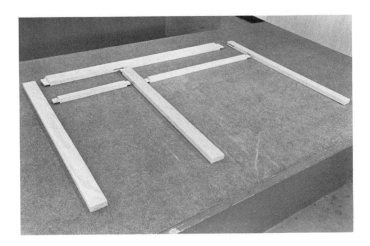

Figure 6-19 Machined face-frame parts ready for assembly

The horizontal (long) cuts for the pull board may be carefully made on the table saw using the following procedure:

1. Draw the location of the pull-board cutout on the face-frame rail. Extend the end lines all the way across the rail as shown in Figure 6-20.
2. Set the table-saw blade at a height that will allow the blade to extend through the face-frame rail by about 1/4 in. Mark the location of the back and front positions of the blade on the rip fence as shown in Figure 6-21.
3. Crank the blade below the table, counting the number of turns of the handle required to lower the blade below the table.
4. Set the rip fence 1 in. away from the blade for the first cut. Position the face-frame rail so that the line representing one end of the opening is in line with the back line drawn on the rip fence (Figure 6-22).

Figure 6-20 Layout for pull-board cut-out

Figure 6-21 Marking the front and rear of the blade on the rip fence

Figure 6-22 Aligning the mark on the face frame with the rear mark on the rip fence

5. Clamp a feather board to the rip fence as shown in Figure 6-23. This will keep the stock from raising off the table when the blade is raised into the wood.

6. Start the saw, and while holding the face-frame rail with the left hand, crank the blade up through the rail to its previous height (counting the turns). Then run the face-frame rail until the mark on the other end of the cutout lines up with the front mark on the rip fence (Figure 6-24).

7. The other horizontal cut is made in the same manner. The end cuts are then made with a saber saw (Figure 6-25).

Figure 6-23 Clamping a feather board to the rip fence

Figure 6-24 Finishing the cut

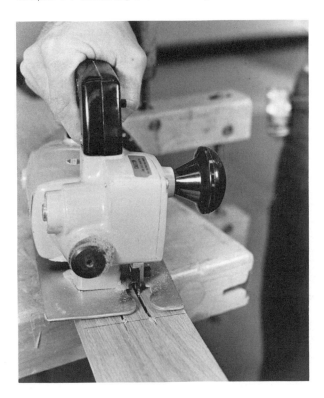

Figure 6-25 Making the end cuts with a saber saw

FACE-FRAME ASSEMBLY

The face-frame parts are glued, clamped, and checked for squareness before being attached to the cabinet. It is a good practice to dry-fit the parts of the first face frame on a job to make sure that all parts fit properly before glue is applied.

If the face frame is assembled face down in the clamps, glue may be applied to the face side of the mortise and the back side of the tenon as shown in Figure 6-26. This will prevent glue from being squeezed out the face side of the joint. Having the face down while clamping leaves the back of the face frame

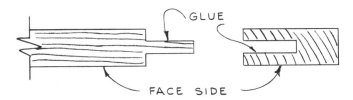

Figure 6-26 Mortise-and-tenon joint showing proper glue placement. Excess glue will not be forced from the face of the joint with this method.

exposed; the tenon may be pinned with short staples from the back so that it may be removed from the clamps immediately (Figure 6-27).

Before the joint is pinned, however, the face frame should be checked for squareness by measuring diagonally from corner to corner (Figure 6-28). Any out of squareness can be easily corrected at this stage by angling the clamps in the direction of the longer diagonal measurement (Figure 6-29).

If a wide-belt sander is available, the face frame may receive a preliminary sanding before being mounted on the cabinet (Figure 6-30). At this point, the face frame is set aside until the cabinet body is assembled.

Figure 6-27 Stapling the back side of the mortise-and-tenon joint

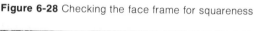

Figure 6-28 Checking the face frame for squareness

Figure 6-29 Placing the clamps at an angle to pull the face frame square

Figure 6-30 Sanding the assembled face frame with a wide-belt sander

Chapter 7

Cabinet Doors

First impressions are important! Most people get their first impression of a set of cabinets from the doors. The doors usually constitute the majority of the visible surface of a set of cabinets, and their styling determines the style of the cabinets. If the exterior surfaces such as doors and drawer fronts are not attractive, very few potential customers will look beyond the surface to see the excellent-quality workmanship and convenience features that you may have built into the cabinets. In remodel work, many otherwise functional cabinets are replaced with new cabinets simply because the homeowner wants to improve the appearance of the house. The cabinetmaker should always consider the appearance of doors and drawer fronts.

Of course, doors also serve functional purposes. They conceal the contents of the cabinet and keep out dust. They may also be equipped with locks to secure the contents of the cabinet. They may have racks, trays, or shelves mounted on their inside surface for additional storage.

In this chapter we discuss the three types of hinged doors and some of the more popular styles of cabinet doors. We then present the construction techniques and procedures for making these doors. We also discuss two nonhinged doors, sliding bypass doors and tambour doors. The procedure for installing doors is covered in Chapter 10.

TYPES OF DOORS

Cabinet doors are often classified according to how they are mounted on the cabinet. The three basic types are lip doors, overlay doors, and flush doors.

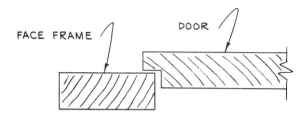

FACE FRAME

DOOR

Figure 7-1 Lip door

The lip door has a rabbet (usually 3/8 in. by 3/8 in.) along the door edges. The lip resulting from the rabbet laps over the face-frame member, as shown in Figure 7-1.

This lip-type door is relatively easy to fit because the lip does not leave a visible gap between the door and the face frame. Figure 7-2 shows a cabinet with a lip-type door.

Overlay doors (Figures 7-3 through 7-5) are mounted on the face-frame surface and cover the door opening. They are sometimes made with a beveled edge that provides a gripping surface for opening the door, thus eliminating the need for door pulls. Overlay doors are also used on cabinets without face frames, as shown in Figure 7-5.

Flush doors are set in the face-frame opening so that the outside surface of the door is flush with the face of the cabinet (Figure 7-6). These doors are much more difficult to fit than the lip or overlay doors because the gap between the door and the face frame is visible. This means that the door must be very accurately fitted within the opening so that the edge gap is uniform. This gap should be about the thickness of a dime. Occasionally, the settling that often occurs in a new house will cause a noticeable difference in the fit of flush doors from the way they were fitted when installed.

Figure 7-2 Cabinet with lip door

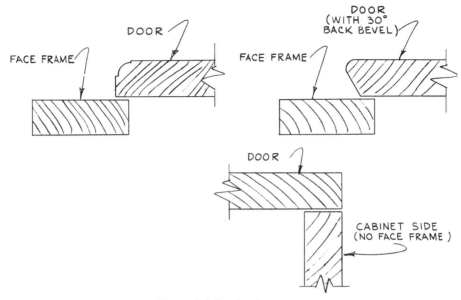

Figure 7-3 Overlay doors

Figure 7-4 Cabinet with overlay doors

Figure 7-5 Cabinets with overlay doors without face frames

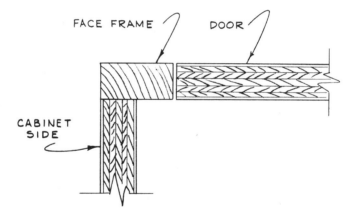

Figure 7-6 Flush door

DOOR STYLES

The simplest cabinet door to make is a flat door. While such doors are not as stylish as some, they are preferred by many people for their "clean," unadorned lines and for ease of cleaning. They are usually made of veneer-core or, occcasionally, lumber-core plywood. Flat doors are rarely made from laminated solid lumber because if its tendency to warp. Figure 7-7 shows a cabinet with flat doors. Notice that the grain is matched between drawer fronts and between door and drawer fronts.

Frame-and-panel doors are very popular for cabinets and furniture. They consist of a frame made up of two stiles, two rails, and a panel (Figure 7-8).

Figure 7-7 Cabinet with flat doors

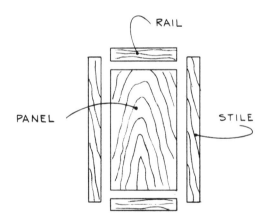

Figure 7-8 Frame-and-panel door components

With frame-and-panel construction, an almost unlimited number of door styles may be developed.

The door frame may be molded to various shapes on the inside edge, outside edge, or both edges. The panel may be flat, flat with V grooves, raised, or carved. The top and bottom rails may be arched or straight. The panel may be made of something other than wood, such as glass, plastic, caning, or expanded metal mesh. Figure 7-9 shows several of the more popular frame-and-panel doors.

Another type of door showing a European influence is the flat door with tongue and groove boards, shown in Figure 7-10. This is in reality a frame-and-

Figure 7-9 Frame-and-panel doors

Figure 7-10 "European" door

panel door whose panel is made of a number of tongue-and-groove-fitted boards.

MAKING FLAT DOORS

Flat doors are usually made from 3/4-in. hardwood plywood to match the cabinet. They are cut to cover the cabinet opening plus a certain amount of the cabinet face frame. Lip doors cover the cabinet face frame 1/4 in. on each lip. Such a door would therefore be cut 1/2 in. wider than the opening to allow for the lip (see "The Cutting List" in Figure 7-11). Note that the door extends over the face frame only 1/4 in. even though the lip on the door is 3/8 in. This leaves 1/8 in. clearance, or a total of 1/4 in. for a door with lips on both edges. The hinges use part of this clearance. The clearance that remains allows some latitude in lining up the doors on the cabinet face.

A cutting list should be made for the doors just as was done for the cabinet in Chapter 5. The drawer fronts are usually cut at the same time as the doors so that they can be grain-matched. Figure 7-11 shows a cabinet drawing and a cutting list for its doors and drawer fronts. Note that the cutting list calls for one large piece to make up the drawer fronts for the bank of drawers. This will later be cut into individual drawer fronts and the pieces kept in sequence so that the grain will match on all the fronts.

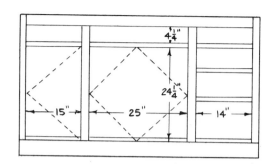

DOOR & DRAWER FRONTS:

1 Pc $\frac{3}{4}$ X 15$\frac{1}{2}$ X 30 (LEFT DOOR & DWR.)
1 Pc $\frac{3}{4}$ X 25$\frac{1}{2}$ X 30 (CENTER)
1 Pc $\frac{3}{4}$ X 14$\frac{1}{2}$ X 30 (RIGHT DWR. FRONTS)

Figure 7-11 Cutting list for plywood lip-type doors and drawer fronts

After developing the cutting list, it is sometimes helpful to lay out a plywood cutting plan on a sheet of paper. This consists of sketching a sheet of plywood to scale, usually 1 in. = 1 ft., and then drawing the cuts on the paper. This is an aid to obtaining the best possible cuttings from the sheet. The cuts should not be drawn directly on the plywood sheet.

The plywood parts are then cut to size on the table saw. When cutting plywood, a very fine–tooth blade made especially for plywood should be used to avoid chipping the face veneers and to provide a smooth cut for the exposed edges. Figure 7-12 shows a carbide-tipped plywood blade and a steel plywood blade. Some table saws are equipped with a small scoring blade ahead of the main cutting blade to eliminate chipping on the underside of the cut.

Figure 7-13 shows the technique to use when making the first cut across the sheet. Note the support rail on the left side of the table saw and the table behind the saw used to support the plywood sheet.

Figure 7-14 shows the technique for cutting a sheet of plywood lengthwise. It is usually advantageous to make cuts across the sheet before making cuts the

Figure 7-12 Carbide-tipped and steel plywood blades

Figure 7-13-a Starting the plywood crosscut. (The saw guard has been removed for clarity in showing the operation.)

Figure 7-13-b Finishing the plywood crosscut

Figure 7-14 Cutting a plywood sheet lengthwise

length of the sheet. If the long narrow pieces are cut first, they are difficult to crosscut safely and accurately on the table saw unless the saw is equipped with a sliding table.

After the doors are cut to finished size, they are then "lipped" by cutting a 3/8-in. by 3/8-in. rabbet on all sides that lip over the face frame. Doors that are in pairs (two doors for one opening) are usually cut in one piece, lipped, and then cut into two doors to avoid accidentally lipping the edge where the two doors join.

There are a number of ways of lipping doors, and the technique used may depend upon the type of equipment available. A table saw may be used with a dado head, as shown in Figure 7-15.

A spindle shaper is probably the most common machine used for lipping doors. A good, sharp carbide cutter is necessary to avoid chipping the face veneer on the plywood (Figure 7-16).

A router mounted on a router table may also be used as shown in Figure 7-17. Again the cutter must be very sharp and should be carbide-tipped. A steel cutter will dull in the area where it is cutting the plywood glue line after just a few cuts.

Figure 7-15 Lipping plywood doors with a dado head on a table saw

Figure 7-16 Lipping doors with a spindle shaper

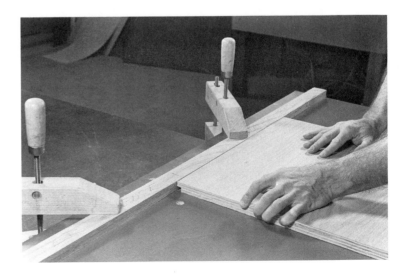

Figure 7-17 Lipping doors with a table-mounted portable router

MAKING FRAME-AND-PANEL DOORS

The frame for a frame-and-panel door is very similar in construction to the face frame discussed in Chapter 6. The stiles and rails may be joined with either mortise-and-tenon joints or with dowels. A simple frame-and-panel door would consist of a frame with a groove around the inside for a 1/4-in. plywood panel. Figure 7-18 shows some typical frame-and-panel shapes used for cabinet doors.

The molded edge shown on the inside edge of the frame members in Figure 7-18 is known as sticking. A number of different sticking shapes may be used to change the appearance of the doors. But such sticking does present a problem in joining the stiles and rails. If the door frame has no molding or sticking as in Figure 7-18a, the door rails may be joined to the stiles with a simple mortise-and-tenon joint or a butt joint with dowels. However, if the stiles have sticking, the rails must be cope-cut to match the sticking (Figure 7-19).

This system of joining door stiles and rails is almost universally used by large-production cabinet shops and furniture manufacturers, whose production molding machines and double-end tenoners are set up to make the mating cuts. This joint can be made in the smaller shop using a spindle shaper and a matched set of cutters. Figure 7-20 shows a shaper built specifically for making doors in which both cutters are mounted on the same shaft. The cabinetmaker runs the stiles and rails through one set of knives to produce the

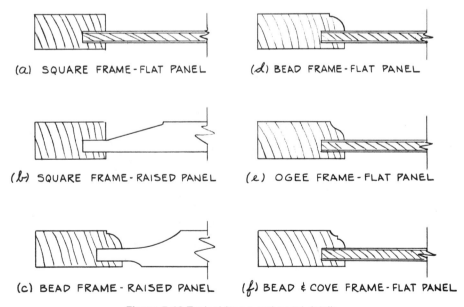

(a) SQUARE FRAME-FLAT PANEL   (d) BEAD FRAME-FLAT PANEL

(b) SQUARE FRAME-RAISED PANEL   (e) OGEE FRAME-FLAT PANEL

(c) BEAD FRAME-RAISED PANEL   (f) BEAD & COVE FRAME-FLAT PANEL

Figure 7-18 Typical frame-and-panel details

Figure 7-19 Cope cut on end of rail to match sticking on the stile

Figure 7-20 Special shaper for making cabinet doors. (Courtesy of the Hammer Machinery Co., Inc., Santa Rosa, Calif.)

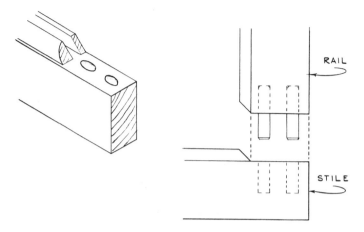

Figure 7-21 Sticking cut away from the stile and mitered to fit the rail sticking

edge sticking and then runs the ends of the rails through the other set to produce the matching cope cut. Notice that the machine has three worktables to utilize three sets of knives on the single spindle.

Several other methods of making stile and rail doors are available to the cabinetmaker who does not want to invest in the matched cutters or who does not have access to a shaper. One technique is to carefully cut the sticking away where the rail joins the stile, leaving a flat surface for a butt joint with dowels (Figure 7-21). Obviously, great care must be exercised in cutting the miter on the sticking. The finished appearance of the face of the door will be the same with this method as with the previously described method of coping the joint.

Another alternative is to assemble the stiles and rails with a miter joint (Figure 7-22). This method neatly eliminates the necessity of coping the joint,

Figure 7-22 Stile and rail assembled with a miter joint

Figure 7-23 Sticking machined by a router after the frame has been assembled. Notice that the sticking is round in the corner.

but it is not without its difficulties. The assembly of a miter joint is more difficult than a butt joint or mortise-and-tenon joint because the joint must be clamped across the width of the door and along its length. The clamps must be uniformly tightened to avoid having the miters "creep."

Another alternative is to assemble the frame and glue a flat panel to the back of it. The sticking is then machined by running a router with a suitable molding cutter around the inside of the frame. The disadvantage of this method is that the panel must be applied to the back of the frame, and some people also object to the rounded corner detail produced by the router, as shown in Figure 7-23.

Yet another method is to make the door frame square (without sticking) and attach a quarter-round or other molding after the door is assembled. These moldings are mitered at the corners and give the appearance of having sticking on the door stiles and rails (Figure 7-24).

Certain styles of doors call for an arched or cathedral top, as shown in Figure 7-25. This is easily accomplished when the sticking is machined with a router as previously described. The top rail is band-sawn to the desired contour, and the pilot bearing on the router is used to follow the contour. When the sticking is machined on the individual stiles and rails with a shaper,

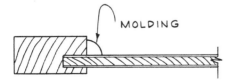

MOLDING

Figure 7-24 Molding applied after the door has been assembled

Figure 7-25 Cathedral-top door

Figure 7-26 Cathedral-top rail being machined on the shaper

Figure 7-27a Raised panel
with straight bevel

Figure 7-27b Raised panel
with cove

depth collars must be used on the spindle to allow the cutter to follow the contour (Figure 7-26).

Fortunately, the door panel is less complex than the door frame. If the panel is to be flat (1/4-in. plywood, glass, plastic, etc.), it is simply cut to size. The other popular option is the raised panel, usually made from laminated solid lumber. The shape of the raised panel is usually either a bevel, as shown in Figure 7-27a, or a cove cut, as shown in Figure 7-27b. These panels are usually made using a spindle shaper with a raised panel cutter. Figure 7-28 shows a cutter for making the cove-shaped cut.

In the absence of a shaper, a suitable raised panel may be made using the table saw. The blade is tilted 15° (a saw in which the blade tilts away from the fence must be used), and the board is run in a vertical position, as shown in Figures 7-29 and 7-30. The panel is then run horizontally to cut the small bevel, as shown in Figure 7-31. All saw marks must then be sanded from the beveled surfaces.

Figure 7-28 Raised-panel
shaper-cutter

Figure 7-29 Cutting a raised panel on the table saw

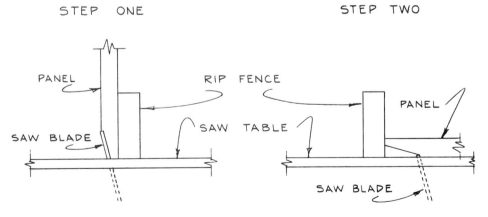

STEP ONE

STEP TWO

PANEL

RIP FENCE

PANEL

SAW BLADE

SAW TABLE

SAW BLADE

Figure 7-30 Cutting a raised panel on the table saw

Figure 7-31 Cutting the small bevel on the raised panel

Once the stiles, rails, and panels have been cut and machined, sanding is done to areas that would be difficult to sand after the door is assembled.

You are now ready to assemble the door. After a trial fitting, glue is applied to the adjoining surfaces, taking care not to get glue on exposed surfaces. The door is then clamped across the rails as shown in Figure 7-32.

Figure 7-32 Clamping a frame-and-panel door

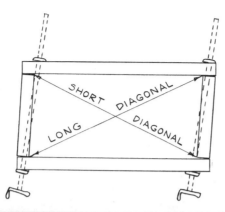

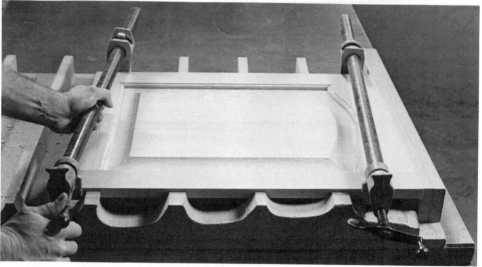

Figure 7-33 Clamps angled to pull the door frame square

As soon as the clamps are tightened, the door must quickly be checked for squareness by measuring diagonally from corner to corner. If the diagonal measurements are not equal, the clamps may be loosened and angled slightly in the direction of the longer diagonal, as shown in Figure 7-33. When they are retightened, the door will be pulled square. In fact, care must be exercised not to pull the door out of square in the opposite direction! A pointed stick of appropriate length (Figure 7-34) works well to check diagonal lengths.

In addition to keeping the door square while gluing, it must also be kept flat. Figure 7-35 shows a simple shop-built fixture for squaring doors and keeping them flat.

If any glue is squeezed from the joint while clamping, it should be left to harden and then be cut from the surface with a sharp knife or chisel rather than

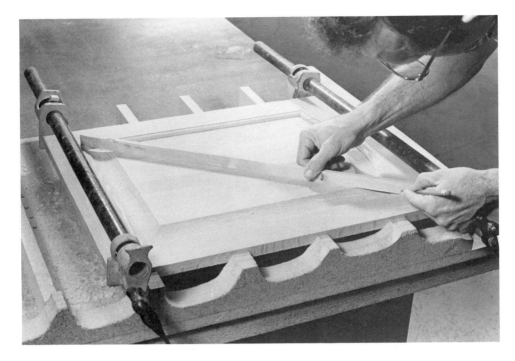

Figure 7-34 Using a stick to check diagonal lengths

Figure 7-35 Fixture for holding doors square for gluing

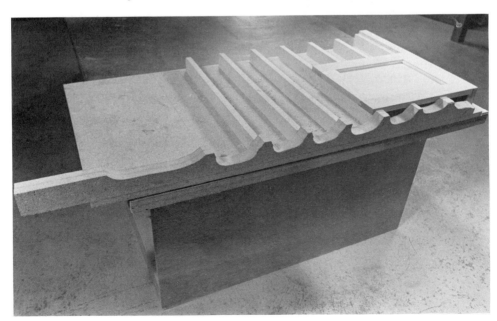

Figure 7-36 Clamp nails such as these may be used to assemble a door frame. (Courtesy of Senco Products, Inc.)

being wiped while wet. Wiping wet glue, even with a wet cloth, will force it into the pores of the wood and will affect the way the wood accepts a finish.

Making attractive frame-and-panel doors is one of the most difficult operations for a small shop to do economically. One method that is fairly simple consists of making the frame, with square edges. The stiles and rails are doweled or may even be butted and assembled with air-driven clamp nails (Figure 7-36).

A 3/8-in. plywood back is then glued and stapled to the back of the frame. This plywood back is 3/4 in. smaller in width and length than the door frame, leaving a 3/8 in. lip. Finally, the inside edge of the frame is molded with a router. Figure 7-37 shows a section of such a door.

The final step before hanging the doors is to sand the assembled doors. The preliminary sanding may be done on a wide-belt sander when one is available

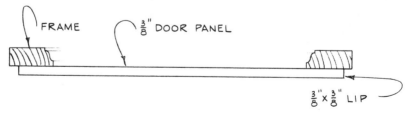

Figure 7-37 Frame-and-panel door with the frame mounted on a plywood panel

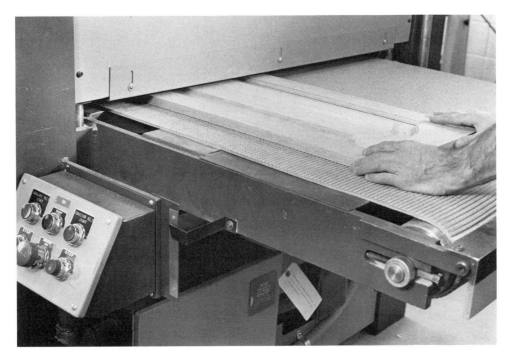

Figure 7-38 Sanding an assembled door with a wide-belt sander

(Figure 7-38). The cross-grain sanding marks will then have to be removed with a finish sander.

The doors may also be sanded with a portable belt sander by first sanding the rails and lightly sanding across the joint (Figure 7-39). The stiles are then sanded, being careful to sand right up to the joint as shown in Figure 7-40. The final sanding is again done with a finishing sander (Figure 7-41).

Figure 7-39 Sanding door rails with a belt sander

Figure 7-40 Sanding the door stiles with a belt sander

Figure 7-41 Final sanding with a finish sander

SLIDING AND TAMBOUR DOORS

Thus far our discussion has dealt only with hinged doors. There are, however, situations where sliding doors are better. They don't require space in front of the cabinet, and when glass doors are required, they eliminate the problems inherent in hinging glass doors. Sliding cabinet doors are usually 1/4-in. plywood, hardboard, glass, or plastic. Figure 7-42 shows a cabinet with sliding doors. Grooved hardwood or plastic track is available and is nailed, stapled, or glued into the cabinet. Occasionally the grooves for the doors may be machined directly into the cabinet top and bottom. The top grooves should be twice as deep as the bottom grooves so that the door can be inserted in the top groove, lifted, and dropped into the bottom groove. Recessed pulls are available for sliding doors.

Another type of sliding door that is sometimes used on cabinets is the tambour door. This door is made from a number of wood slats held together with a canvas backing. This gives it a flexibility that will allow it to slide along a curved track. Its operation is similar to that of a roll-top desk. The track usually runs along the front of the cabinet and then along the side (Figure 7-43). This allows the entire front of the cabinet to be open, as opposed to sliding doors, which allow only one side to be open at a time.

Figure 7-44 shows a cabinet with tambour doors.

Figure 7-42 Cabinet with sliding doors

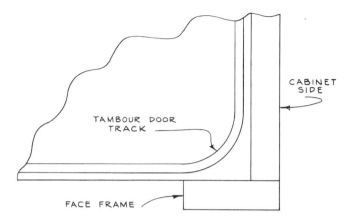

Figure 7-43 Groove cut on cabinet top and bottom for sliding tambour doors.

(a)

(b)

Figure 7-44 Cabinet with tambour doors

Chapter 8

Drawers and Drawer Guide Systems

Drawers provide the most efficient storage for many items and should be used whenever possible. However, they do present some construction problems. They must be strong enough to withstand pulling on the drawer front with an item jammed inside the drawer, yet they should not be unduly heavy. They must be accurately fitted so that they slide without an excess of lateral (sideways) motion, yet must not be so tight that they stick. To compound the problem, when the drawer and cabinet are made of wood, they are both subject to shrinking and swelling with changes in humidity, so the drawer guide system must allow for this.

Some drawers are used for storing heavy objects such as tools or small appliances and must be designed accordingly. In this chapter we look at methods of overcoming these problems.

DRAWER TYPES AND STYLES

Drawers are made to fit the cabinet, using either lip, overlay, or flush construction, just as are the doors (Chapter 7). Their construction usually matches that of the doors. Figure 8-1 shows a plan view of drawers that use each of the three fitting methods.

The style of the drawer front is also designed to match that of the doors, except that frame-and-panel construction is rarely used for drawer fronts. Where frame-and-panel construction is used on doors, the drawer fronts are

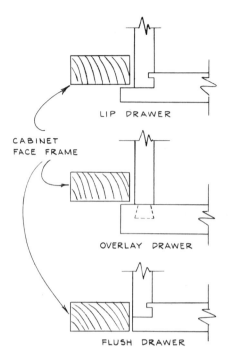

LIP DRAWER

CABINET
FACE FRAME

OVERLAY DRAWER

FLUSH DRAWER

Figure 8-1 Drawer-front fitting methods

made of a matching solid wood and the outside edge is shaped to match that of the door.

When flat plywood is used for the doors, it is also used for the drawer fronts. In this case, the grain is usually run vertically and is matched from one drawer to the next.

DRAWER DESIGN AND CONSTRUCTION

The materials used in drawer construction are usually as follows:

1. *Front:* 3/4-in. hardwood or hardwood plywood
2. *Sides:* 1/2-in. hardwood, softwood, plywood, or medium-density fiberboard
3. *Backs:* 1/2-in. or 3/4-in. hardboard, softwood, plywood, or particle board
4. *Bottom:* 1/4-in. plywood or hardboard

One of the major factors in determining the strength of a drawer is the type of joint selected for joining the sides to the front and back. The joint between the front and sides is especially critical because the force of pulling the drawer open is transferred through this joint. Some of the joints commonly used to assemble drawers are shown in Figure 8-2.

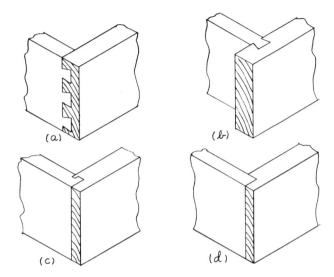

Figure 8-2 Typical joints used for joining drawer fronts to drawer sides: (a) dovetail, (b) dovetail dado, (c) double dado, (d) rabbet

Of the joints shown, the dovetail and dovetail dado are strongest and should be used where heavy loads or hard use is anticipated. The double dado is acceptable for most cabinet construction, and the rabbet is used when lighter loads are anticipated. A butt joint is sometimes used to join the back to the sides in light construction. A dado or rabbet joint may also be used. The drawer bottom is usually set in a groove in the drawer sides and fronts.

MACHINING DRAWER JOINTS

Dovetail joints are made on special dovetail machines in large production shops. In smaller shops they are made using a dovetail cutting accessory for a portable router. The drawer front and mating side are machined together in one operation. Figure 8-3 shows dovetail joints being made this way.

The dovetail dado also uses the portable router. The dovetail groove is cut with a protable router or an overarm router, as shown in Figure 8-4. The dovetail tongue is cut on the table saw by making the shoulder cut first and then making the bevel cuts, as shown in Figure 8-5.

The double dado joint may be made on the table saw. The first step is to make a rabbet on the end of the drawer front, as shown in Figure 8-6.

The second step is to cut out the shaded area shown in Figure 8-6 by running the drawer front over the table saw in a vertical position (Figure 8-7). The final step is to cut a matching dado in the drawer side (Figure 8-8).

There are several drawer-making machines available with matched sets of cutters for machining joints on drawer components. Figure 8-9 shows such a

Figure 8-3 Cutting a dovetail joint

Figure 8-4 Cutting a dovetail dado with the overarm router

Figure 8-5-a Making the shoulder cuts for a dovetail using the table saw

Figure 8-5-b Making the dovetail face cut

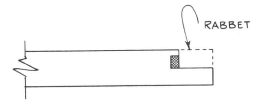

Figure 8-6 Rabbet cut for a double dado drawer joint. (The shaded area will be removed next.)

Figure 8-7 Finishing the double dado on the table saw

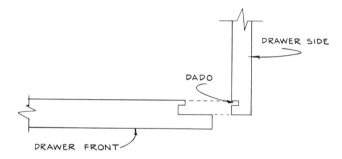

Figure 8-8 Machine work completed for double dado drawer joint

Figure 8-9 Drawer-making machine. (Courtesy of the Hammer Machinery Co., Inc., Santa Rosa, Calif.)

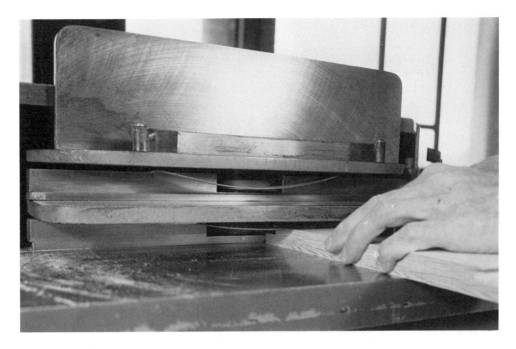

Figure 8-10 Cutting a double dado joint on the drawer-making machine

machine for making the double dado joint for assembling drawer fronts, sides, and backs. It also has cutters for lipping doors and drawer fronts, grooving for drawer bottoms, and rounding the edges of drawer fronts. Such a machine speeds up the drawer-making process greatly. Figure 8-10 shows a double dado joint being made on this machine.

A final machining operation that is sometimes performed on drawer components is to slightly round or "relieve" the top edge of the drawer sides. This is usually done on a shaper.

In summary, the process for making drawer parts is as follows:

1. Cut all the component parts to exact size. The size of the parts relative to the drawer opening will vary according to the guide system being used. (Guide systems are discussed later in this chapter.)
2. Machine joints for joining drawer front to drawer sides and for joining back to sides.
3. Machine a 3/8-in. lip on drawer front if lip construction is being used.
4. Machine a 1/4-in. groove in the drawer front and sides for the drawer bottom.
5. Relieve the top edge of the drawer sides (optional).
6. Machine any decorative molding desired on the drawer front.
7. Assemble the drawer as described in the following section.

DRAWER ASSEMBLY

Drawers assembled with dovetail or dovetail dado joints are usually glued and clamped. Care must be taken to keep the drawer flat (avoid twisting) and square while being glued. The diagonal measurements should be checked as described in Chapter 7 for door assembly.

Drawers using the double dado or rabbet joint are usually glued and nailed or stapled together. Figure 8-11 shows a convenient sequence for assembling such a drawer. Notice the stop block clamped to the bench to keep the drawer parts from sliding while they are being nailed. They may also be assembled with an air nailer or stapler.

Figure 8-11-a Nailing one drawer side to the drawer front

Figure 8-11-b Nailing the second side to the front

Figure 8-11-c Attaching the drawer back

Figure 8-11-d Inserting the drawer bottom

Figure 8-11-e Nailing the
drawer bottom to the back

Figure 8-11-f The assembled drawer

DRAWER GUIDE SYSTEMS

One of the most popular drawer guide systems used in residential cabinet work is the wood center guide. The basic component of this system is a wood guide rail running from the front to the rear of the cabinet under the center of the drawer, as shown in Figure 8-12. When this system is used, it must be accompanied by a similar rail above the drawer (Figure 8-13) to keep the drawer from tipping down when pulled more than halfway out. This rail is called a tip rail or kicker. The wood guide is usually used in conjunction with a set of hard nylon guide tabs that locate and guide the drawer along the wood guide rail.

Figure 8-12 Drawer center guide

Figure 8-13 Drawer tip rail

A set of these nylon guides consists of a plastic tab for the left and right side of the drawer opening (Figure 8-14), a U-shaped tab that mounts under the back of the drawer to slide on the bottom rail, and a tab that mounts on the top of the drawer back (Figure 8-15) to slide against the tip rail.

Figure 8-14 Plastic guide tabs may be used in the corners of the drawer opening.

Figure 8-15 Plastic guide mounted on the drawer bottom. This guide slides on the wood center guide rail shown in Figure 8-12.

This system requires that the drawer be 1/4 in. less in width and height than the drawer opening (1/8 in. on each side) to allow for the plastic tabs.

The wood center guide is usually made of hardwood and is 3/4 in. thick by 1 3/8 in. wide. The actual width is determined by the width of the front-face frame rail (usually 1 in.) and by the distance of the drawer bottom from the bottom of the drawer side (usually 3/8 in.). The length of the drawer guide is equal to the inside depth of the cabinets plus 3/8 in.

The center guide is attached to the cabinet by first cutting a 1-in. by 5/8-in. rabbet across one end and attaching a 1/4-in. by 1-in. by approximately 3-in. plywood tab, as shown in Figure 8-16. This guide is then centered in the drawer opening. The 1/4-in. plywood tab is glued and nailed or stapled from inside the cabinet to the face frame (Figure 8-17).

The back end of the guide is not attached to the cabinet until the drawer is ready to be fitted. After the center guide is attached to the front of the cabinet and the plastic tabs are in place, the drawer may be fitted by reaching into the cabinet and supporting the drawer guide with one hand while sliding the drawer into the opening with the other. With the drawer completely closed, the rear of the guide rail may be moved up, down, or sideways to get the best possible fit of the drawer front against the face of the cabinet (Figure 8-18).

Once you have attained a good fit on the drawer, you may staple through the back of the cabinet into the drawer guide with your third hand, or you may have an assistant do it!

Center guide rails are sometimes also used with a hardwood guide, mounted under the drawer, that has a groove that matches the width of the guide rail (Figure 8-19). This would replace the plastic tabs.

Another guide system sometimes used consists of hardwood side guides mounted to the cabinet on either side of the drawer opening and corresponding grooves in the drawer sides (Figure 8-20). This system eliminates the need for a

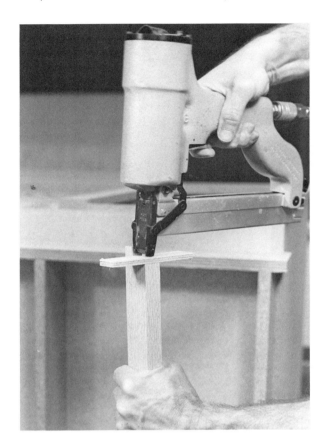

Figure 8-16 Attaching a 1/4-in. plywood tab to a center guide rail before the rail is installed

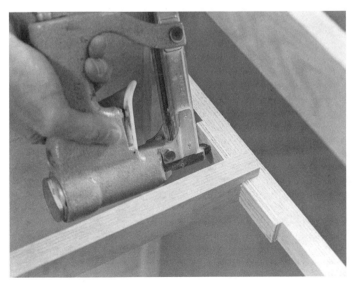

Figure 8-17 The 1/4-in. plywood tab is then glued and stapled to the face-frame rail from inside the cabinet.

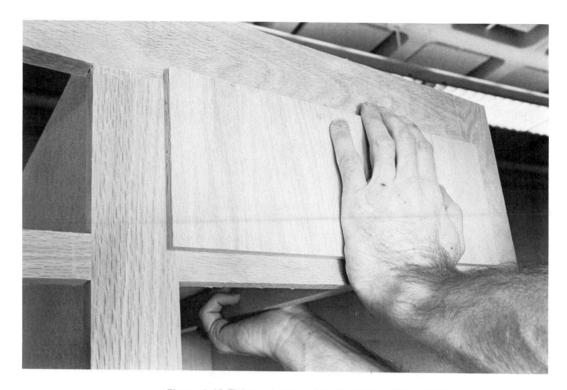

Figure 8-18 Fitting a drawer using the center guide system

Figure 8-19 Grooved hardwood guide on the underside of a drawer to match the center guide rail

Figure 8-20 Hardwood side guides

Figure 8-21 Center roller guides

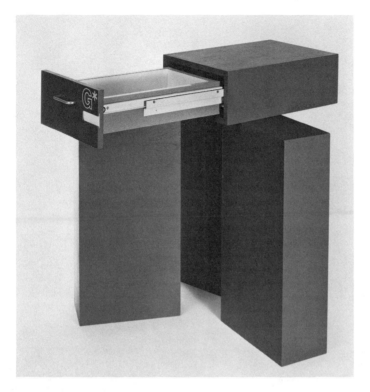

Figure 8-22 Side roller guides. (Courtesy of Grass America, Inc., Kernersville, North Carolina)

separate tip rail, but it is somewhat more difficult to fit. However, when properly fitted and waxed, it allows the drawer to slide very smoothly.

There are, of course, a number of commercially made roller guide systems as described in Chapter 3. These vary a great deal in cost and ease of installation. Center roller guides (Figure 8-21) are fairly inexpensive and are used for low-load applications. Most of the better side guide systems, such as those shown in Figure 8-22, are very smooth in operation, and some of them are rated at 75 lb. load capacity or higher. These generally require 1/2 in. on each side of the drawer (the drawer must be 1 in. narrower than the opening), and they may require extra structural work inside the cabinet to provide a mounting surface flush with the inside edge of the drawer opening.

ROLL-OUT TRAYS

A modified drawer, called a roll-out tray, is often used in place of shelves in base cabinets. Since the roll-out tray is normally hidden behind the cabinet doors, the front is not necessarily made to match the cabinet faces but rather of the same material as the drawer sides. The front is often narrower than the sides, as shown in Figure 8-23, to provide easy access to the contents. Roll-out

Figure 8-23 Roll-out trays

trays are usually mounted on side roller guides, but hardwood side guides may also be used. Notice that false partitions are installed just inside the door opening for mounting the roller guides. This allows the trays to be rolled out past the doors even when they are opened only 90°.

Chapter 9

Cabinet Cutout and Machining

Cabinet cutout and machining consists of cutting all of the parts on the cutting list (see Chapter 5) to finished size and then machining all joints, moldings, and other parts as specified in the shop drawings. Before cutting begins, the cutting list should be studied carefully to determine the best utilization of material. When cutting hardwood plywoods, it is sometimes helpful to sketch the proposed cutting plan on a piece of paper to obtain the best utilization of the 4-ft. by 8-ft. sheet.

Most of the cutting of sheet materials is done on the table saw. Hardwood plywoods are particularly sensitive to chipping when cutting across the face grain, so it is very important that a sharp plywood blade be fitted for cutting sheet material. The table surface, rip fence, and the bars that the rip fence slides on should all be waxed with a hard paste wax and buffed before starting to cut. When running large sheets of plywood or particle board through the saw, any binding caused by friction between the wood and the fence or table surface could cause the wood to bind against the saw blade and be kicked back at the operator. The wood will slide smoothly on the waxed surface, and this also reduces operator fatigue.

MEASUREMENTS AND ACCURACY

Accuracy in measuring is critical in cabinetmaking. Most cabinets have a specific location into which they must fit. It is not uncommon to have three or four or more cabinets in a row, and the total length of all the cabinets must not

Figure 9-1 A table saw with a measuring scale for setting the rip fence. (Courtesy of Biesemeyer Manufacturing Corporation)

vary more than 1/16 in. Each of these cabinets is made of a number of parts that must be cut accurately if the total specified cabinet dimensions are to be maintained.

Many table saws have a measuring scale built into the rail that the rip fence slides on (Figure 9-1). These are very helpful in cabinetmaking because they allow the rip fence to be quickly changed for different-width cuts without shutting off the saw, waiting for the blade to stop, and then measuring the blade-to-fence distance.

They should, however, be checked for accuracy before relying on them for accurate measurement. For instance, any time a different blade is installed, the fence should be adjusted (Figure 9-2).

When the fence must be set by measuring, a steel measuring tape may be used. The tip of the tape is placed against the rip fence, as shown in Figure 9-3, and the tape blade is run directly under a sawtooth that points toward the fence. The actual measurement is taken from the fence side of the tooth. Ac-

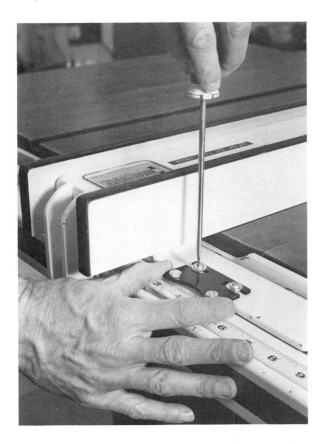

Figure 9-2 "Zeroing" the rip fence measuring scale

Figure 9-3 Setting the rip fence by measuring

curacy here is important because the distance between the inside of the blade and the rip fence determines the size of the part being cut.

HANDLING SHEET MATERIALS ON THE TABLE SAW

Handling and cutting a 4-ft. by 8-ft. sheet of plywood on a table saw is intimidating at first, but it need not be difficult. Most table saw tops are not large enough to support the sheet completely while it is being cut and after it has been cut into two pieces. A simple rail to the left of the saw and a table behind the saw, as shown in Figure 9-4, can easily be built to allow a person to cut plywood without assistance. This rail and table are at saw-table height and can be moved out of the way when not needed. On smaller saws it is helpful to extend the rip fence also (Figure 9-5). If the saw is used only for cutting sheet material, a larger table surface may be attached to the saw.

When cutting across the sheet, the operator should stand near the center of the sheet or slightly to the left, as shown in Figure 9-6. The sheet is pushed against the rip fence, and the cut is started. The operator must watch carefully

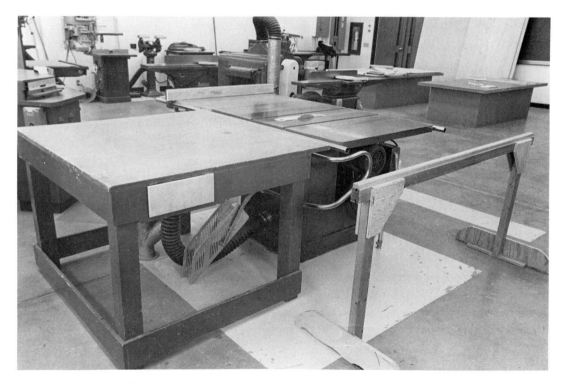

Figure 9-4 A support rail and off-bearing table make cutting large plywood sheets easier.

Figure 9-5 Extended rip fence for a small table saw

Figure 9-6 The operator should stand near the center of the sheet when crosscutting plywood on the table saw. (The saw guard has been removed for clarity in showing this operation.)

Figure 9-7 Completing the plywood crosscut. The piece between the blade and the rip fence must be pushed completely past the rear of the blade before it is released.

Figure 9-8 Cutting a plywood sheet in the long direction

to see that the end of the sheet stays against the rip fence. As the cut is completed, the operator moves toward the rip fence and pushes the piece between the blade and the fence past the back of the blade (Figure 9-7). Just as the cut is completed, the operator reduces the pressure on the part to the left of the blade so that it doesn't bind on the blade.

Making cuts in the long direction of the sheet is much easier. The operator guides the sheet from the back, as shown in Figure 9-8. Again, it is important to see that the edge of the sheet stays firmly against the rip fence.

CUTTING CABINET PARTS TO SIZE

In this section of the chapter, and in the next section on machining operations, we go step-by-step through the process of cutting out a set of cabinets. The exact sequence of operation may vary somewhat according to the job and the equipment available.

Before cutting is started, the cutting list should be studied carefully. Each cabinet on the list might have some parts that are identical. These should all be cut at the same time to save time in changing the saw settings. Larger parts should generally be cut first; smaller parts are then cut from the remaining material.

The series of photographs in Figure 9-9 shows a typical sequence for cutting out a set of cabinets, starting with the base cabinets.

Figure 9-9-a Cutting finished ends to length from a large sheet (usually 35 1/4 in. long)

Figure 9-9-b Cutting finished ends to width. (usually 23 1/4 in.) *Note:* These parts are often cut 1/4 in. oversize and then trimmed to finished size to remove the original factory edge, which may be damaged from shipping and handling.

Figure 9-9-c Cutting the bottom and fixed shelf to length

Figure 9-9-d Cutting the bottom and shelf to width (usually 22 3/4 in.)

Figure 9-9-e Cutting the ends for wall cabinets to width

Figure 9-9-f Cutting finished ends to length on the radial-arm saw. Notice the stop block used to cut multiple parts to length.

Figure 9-10 Set of cabinet parts ready for machining

All the parts for the set of cabinets are cut in similar fashion. As each part is cut, it should be marked on the edge so that it may be easily identified. For instance, a finished end for cabinet A might be marked "A–F.E.," or a partition for cabinet E could be marked "E–Part." As each part is cut and marked, it should be set with other parts for the same cabinet. When all the parts for the job are cut out, there will be a stack of parts for cabinet A, another stack for B, and so on. This makes it easy to find parts for the machining operation to be performed next. It also makes it easy for the person assembling the cabinets if all of the parts for each cabinet are grouped together. Figure 9-10 shows a typical set of cabinet parts waiting to be machined.

MACHINING OPERATIONS

The photographs in Figure 9-11 show most of the common machining operations necessary for a typical set of cabinets.

Figure 9-11-a Mitering the front edge of the toe-board cutout on a finished end. Note that the saw blade is set very high for this operation only, to avoid "undercutting" on the back side. The blade should be returned to normal height as soon as this operation is completed.

Figure 9-11-b Cutting the 1/2-in. by 1/2-in. rabbet on the finished end for a base cabinet. (The wall-cabinet finished ends should be run at the same time.)

Figure 9-11-c Notching a partition for the 3/4-in. by 2 1/2-in. nailing strip

Figure 9-11-d Rabbeting the wall-cabinet finished end for the cabinet bottom

Figure 9-11-e Dadoing the finished end for the cabinet top

Figure 9-11-f Cutting the groove for the adjustable shelf standard. Note that these grooves are usually set approximately 1 in. from the front or back of the cabinet for each 10 in. of cabinet depth. The groove for a 12-in.-deep upper cabinet is usually 1 1/4 in. from the front and back of the cabinet.

Figure 9-11-g Cutting the miter joint for joining a finished end to a finished back. Note the piece of scrap wood clamped to the rip fence for the saw blade to cut into.

Figure 9-11-h Cutting a 1/8-in. groove for a spline for joining two pieces of 3/4-in. plywood for a large finished back. Note the feather board clamped to the saw table to hold the plywood tightly against the fence. This ensures that the faces of the adjoining sheets of plywood will be flush with the spline installed.

Figure 9-11-i Two sheets of plywood ready to be edge-joined with a 1/8-in. hardboard spline

Figure 9-11-j Cutting 3/8-in. by 3/4-in. edge banding for shelves and cabinet bottoms. Notice the push stick held against the rip fence and run through the saw to push the thin, 3/8-in. strip past the rear of the blade before releasing it.

MACHINING MOLDINGS

While most cabinets have very few molded or shaped surfaces, some of the more ornate cabinets have a number of molded edges typical of those found in some types of fine furniture. Countertops may have a wood molding around the edges, doors and drawer fronts may be shaped, and door panels may be shaped.

Moldings or shaped edges are usually made in the smaller shop with a spindle shaper, a portable router, or an overarm router. Molding may be made on the shaper using cutters manufactured to stock molding patterns such as those shown in Figure 9-12. These are usually available in high-speed steel or carbide, which is more expensive but stays sharp much longer. Flat knives held in place by grooved collars, as shown in Figure 9-13, may also be used. These knives may be ground to any pattern desired. (Accurate knife grinding is very difficult without specialized equipment and is not covered in this book.)

Figure 9-14 shows an edge being molded on the shaper. If a wide laminated board is to have the edges shaped, the end-grain surfaces should

Figure 9-12 Three-wing shaper-cutters used for making moldings

Figure 9-13 Flat shaper knives held in place with a special set of grooved collars

Figure 9-14 Making a molding on the shaper

always be done first (Figure 9-15). This way, if any splitting occurs at the end of the cut, as it often does on end-grain cutting, the damaged area will usually be cut away when the edge is shaped. It is even a good practice to have the laminated board 1/4 in. to 1/2 in. wider than its finished width before shaping the ends. It can then be cut down to finished width, cutting off any chipped corners before shaping the edges.

The shaper may also be used for shaping curved surfaces when a depth collar is used on the spindle to guide the stock. The collar determines how deep the cutter will be able to cut into the wood. These depth collars are available in incremental sizes to match most cutters. Figure 9-16 shows a depth collar that allows the full molding pattern of the cutter to be used.

When using the shaper to shape a curved surface, a support pin is placed in the table. The stock is supported against this pin and pivoted into the cutter to start the cut (Figure 9-17). As the board comes to rest against the depth collar, the board is moved away from the support pin, and the cut is completed by running the entire edge past the cutter, keeping it against the depth collar.

Portable routers are also often used for machining molded edges. They are especially convenient for use on curved edges since they will easily follow even

Figure 9-15 Running the end grain first

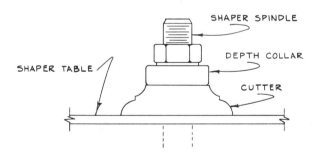

Figure 9-16 Depth collar used on a spindle shaper for shaping curved edges

sharp curves. The router bits used for moldings usually have a pilot bushing that rides against the edge of the board to guide the router, or they may have a small ball bearing for this purpose (Figure 9-18).

To cut a molding with the router, install the desired bit, hold the router flat on the board to be molded, and start the router with the cutter away from the edge. Bring the cutter into the wood until the pilot contacts the edge of the board. Move the router along the edge at a uniform rate, keeping the pilot in

Figure 9-17 Starting a curved cut using a support pin

Figure 9-18 Typical router bits used for molding edges

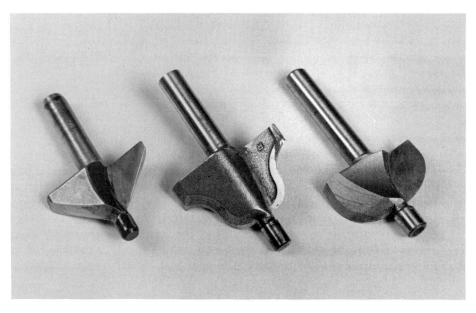

contact with the edge of the board (Figure 9-19). Avoid moving too slowly or stopping; the cutter will quickly overheat and burn the wood.

The normal direction of feed is from left to right as you face the board. However, when it is necessary to run against the grain, chipping can be minimized by going in the other direction. Caution must be observed when doing so because the router will tend to pull itself into the cut. Take a light cut and keep a firm grip on the router.

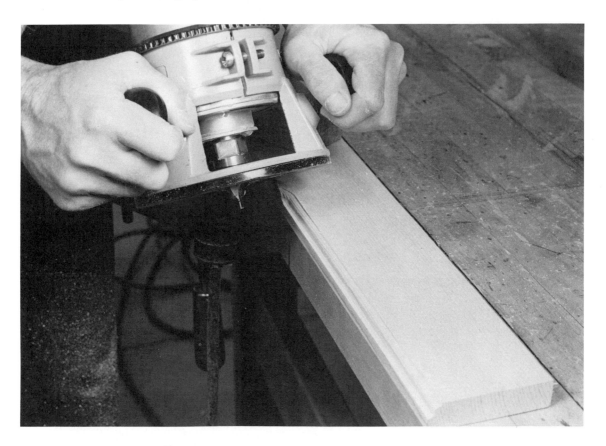

Figure 9-19 Machining a molded edge with a portable router

The overhead or overarm router (Figure 9-20) may also be used for machining molded edges. The same bits may be used except that it is not necessary to have a pilot on the bit for most operations. Figure 9-21 shows a molding being run on a straight edge with a fence guide clamped to the router table. Notice that the cutter is partially "buried" in the guide fence. This acts as a chip breaker. Curved edges may be routed using the router bit with a pilot or by using a pin in the table under the bit that serves as a guide (Figure 9-22).

Figure 9-20 Overarm router

Figure 9-21 Machining a molding on the overarm router

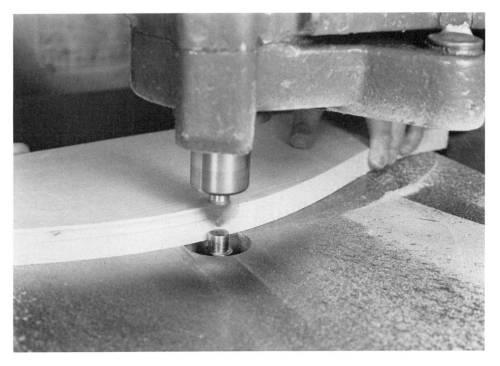

Figure 9-22 Using a guide pin for shaping curved surfaces on the overhead router

MACHINE SAFETY GUIDELINES

Woodworking machines have been improved a great deal in the area of safety in recent years. However, many of them have large, sharp cutters driven by powerful motors and can be dangerous if not used properly. It is probably not possible to list safety rules for every possible operation, but the following guidelines apply to almost all general cutting and machining operations. The equipment manufacturers provide guards with their machines, and while it may occasionally be necessary to remove a guard for a special operation, it should always be replaced immediately upon completion of the operation.

Loose clothing should not be worn when working around machinery. Long shirttails are especially dangerous around a jointer, for example. Long hair should be confined.

It is always possible that chips, loose knots, or other material may be thrown from a machine, so it is important that safety glasses always be worn while woodworking.

Here are some safety rules that must be observed while operating woodworking machines.

Table Saw

1. Any stock to be cut must have a straight edge to run against the rip fence or to place against the miter gauge.
2. The bottom surface of the stock must be flat to prevent it from rocking and binding on the saw blade.
3. The saw blade should be set only 1/8 in. to 1/4 in. above the stock being cut.
4. A push stick should be used to push narrow stock between the blade and the fence. The stock between the blade and the fence must be pushed past the *rear* of the blade before being released.
5. The rip fence must not be used as a guide when crosscutting with the miter gauge. This will leave the part that has been cut trapped between the fence and the blade, and if it rotates, putting pressure against the side of the blade, it will be kicked back violently.
6. The rip fence should never be used as a guide for cutting across narrow stock.
7. Never cut freehand on the table saw. Always use a rip fence or miter gauge to guide the stock being cut.
8. Do not reach over the moving blade to pick up material.
9. The saw blade should be sharp and of the proper type for the cut being made. A fine-toothed crosscut blade or plywood blade, for example, will overheat and bind in the wood when used for ripping heavy, solid stock and may kick the material out of the machine.

Jointer

1. A push block should always be used when face-jointing boards. Never put your hands directly over the cutters.
2. Stock being jointed must be long enough to span the gap between the infeed and outfeed table safely. The minimum safe length for most jointers is 12 in.
3. Check the depth of cut before starting. A very deep cut, especially when face-jointing, increases the likelihood of a kickback.

Shaper

1. Many shapers have a reversing switch so that the spindle can be rotated in either direction. The rotation direction must always be known, and the stock must be fed against the rotation of the cutter.
2. Whenever possible, the machine should be set up so that the cut is being made on the underside of the stock rather than on the top side.
3. Use spring hold-down guides or feather boards when shaping thin or narrow stock.
4. When shaping a contoured edge using a depth collar, a guide pin in the table must be used for starting the work.
5. Do not use material shorter than 12 in.

Radial-Arm Saw

1. The radial-arm saw, when used for crosscutting, is the only circular woodworking saw that feeds in the direction of blade rotation rather than against the direction of blade rotation. This means that the saw tends to pull itself into the wood, so a very firm grip must be maintained on the saw handle to control the rate of cut.

2. The material being cut should be held firmly against the fence and should lay flat on the table.

3. The saw should be pulled smoothly through the board and fully returned before moving the stock being cut.

4. The radial-arm saw is seldom used for ripping stock in cabinet shops. However, if it is necessary to use it for that purpose, it is imperative that the material be fed *against* the rotation of the blade (from the side opposite the antikickback dogs) and that a push stick be used for narrow cuts. The antikickback dogs must be set at the proper height.

Surface Planer

The surface planer is not a particularly dangerous machine. There are, however, a few safety precautions.

1. If the machine has a solid infeed roll and chip breaker as opposed to a sectional feed roll and chip breaker, only one piece of material should be fed at a time. Otherwise, if two boards of different thickness are fed together, the thicker board will raise the infeed roll and chip breaker, allowing the cutter to kick the thin board back out of the machine.

2. Never get down to look in the machine while it is running. A loose knot or other material could be thrown out.

3. The minimum length of stock that can be planed is determined by the distance between the infeed and outfeed rolls.

Band Saw

1. The sliding upper guide assembly should be set so that the guide is about 1/4 in. above the work.

2. The sequence of cuts should be planned to avoid having to back out of curved cuts. This prevents the likelihood of pulling the blade off the wheels.

3. Round stock should not be cut unless it is held in a clamp or a jig to prevent it from rotating while being cut.

4. Do not cut curves with a radius too small for the width of the blade. This will overheat the blade and cause metal fatigue, leading to early blade breakage.

Chapter 10

Cabinet Assembly

Cabinets are usually assembled using glue and pneumatically driven staples and nails. The staples generally have better holding power than nails, but they leave a larger hole in the surface of the wood, so their use is usually restricted to places that are not visible on the finished product. Finish nails are used for attaching face frames to the cabinet and other visible applications where the nail hole must be small and easily filled. Some classes of cabinets, such as Architectural Woodwork Institute premium grade, do not allow nails in face frames.

Pneumatic nailers and staplers have made cabinet assembly much easier and faster. However, there are potential safety hazards involved when using them. The operator's hands should always be well clear of the muzzle. The operator's hands should not be in such a position that they would be hit by a nail deflected out of the board (Figure 10-1). The guns exhaust a blast of air each time they are fired; the operator should know where they exhaust and stay away from that area.

ASSEMBLING THE BASE CABINET

When all the cabinet component parts have been cut and all machine work has been completed, the cabinet is ready for assembly. A large, flat, low (approximately 24 in. high) bench is very convenient for assembling cabinets. The photographs in Figure 10-2 show the assembly sequence for a typical base

Figure 10-1 Using a pneumatic nailer. Hands must be kept clear in case a nail or staple is deflected out of the wood.

cabinet. Most of the photographs show the use of pneumatic staplers and nailers, but the process is the same for hand nailing. Glue is used in all joints.

A 4-in. base block is attached to the finished end to support the cabinet bottom (Figure 10-2a). The cabinet body is then assembled face down on the bench. The cabinet bottom is attached to the base block on the finished end (Figure 10-2b). The other end is attached to the cabinet bottom (Figure 10-2c). If the cabinet has a partition, it is attached to the bottom. Note, if the cabinet has a fixed shelf, the shelf can serve as a spacer to locate the partition, as in the photograph in Figure 10-2d.

The shelf is then attached to the end and the partition (Figure 10-2e). Note the 1/4-in. plywood spacers used to locate the shelf at the proper height (usually 11 in. from the bottom of the cabinet).

Figure 10-2-a Attaching 4-in. base blocks to a finished end

Figure 10-2-b Attaching the bottom

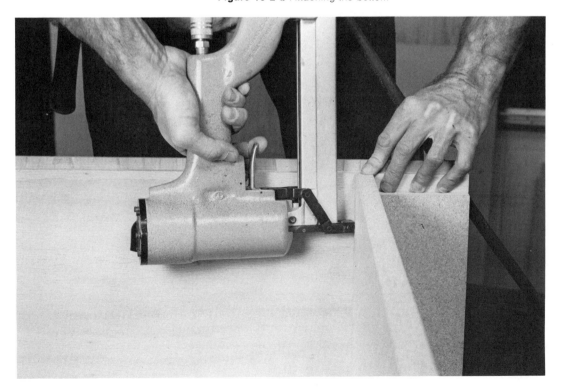

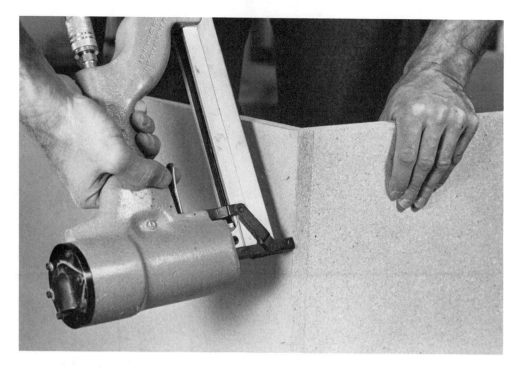

Figure 10-2-c Attaching the other (wall) end to the bottom

Figure 10-2-d Attaching the partition. The shelf is used as a spacer to locate the partition.

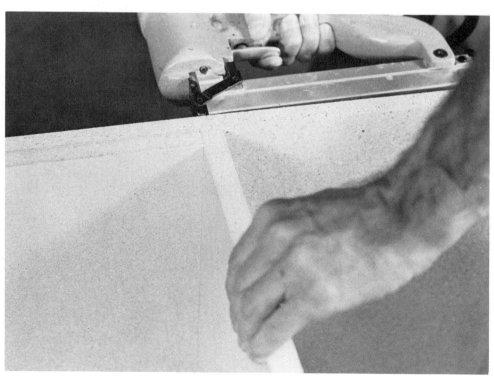

Figure 10-2-e Attaching the shelf to the end and the partition using plywood spacers for location

The nailing strip is attached next (Figure 10-2f). Then the base is assembled (Figure 10-2g) and attached to the back of the cabinet (Figure 10-2h). It will be attached to the front of the cabinet later. Note the 2 1/4-in. spacer blocks used to hold the base in position while it is being attached to the cabinet.

The back is attached next (Figure 10-2i). The back is used to square the cabinet, so the back must be checked for squareness. The back is first nailed or stapled to one end of the cabinet. Then it is pulled up or down as necessary to make its top edge line up with the top edge of the cabinet, as shown in Figure 10-2j. This squares the cabinet.

The back is then nailed to the cabinet bottom, partition, and fixed shelf. A square or chalk line is used to locate the center of partitions and shelves for nailing purposes (Figure 10-2k).

The cabinet is now turned over on its back for final assembly. The face frame is attached first (Figure 10-2 1). Great care must be taken to hold the edge of the face frame flush with any finished ends. As soon as the face frame is nailed to the cabinet, the joint between the face frame and the finished end should be examined carefully. If it is not completely tight, it should be clamped

Figure 10-2-f Attaching the nailing strip

Figure 10-2-g Assembling the cabinet base

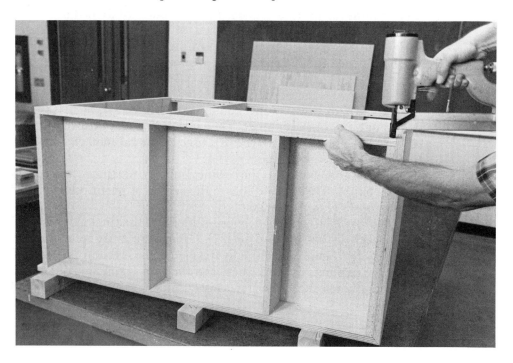

Figure 10-2-h Attaching the base
to the back side of the cabinet

Figure 10-2-i Attaching the cabinet back to one end of the cabinet

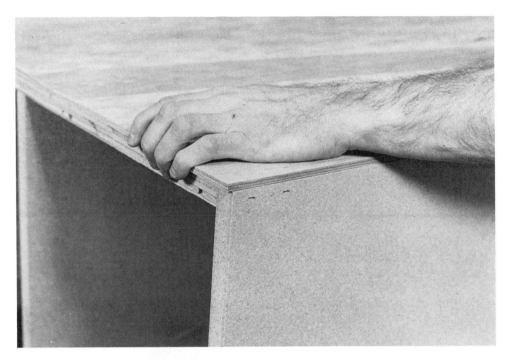

Figure 10-2-j Using the back to square the cabinet

Figure 10-2-k Using a square to locate the center of the partition for nailing

Figure 10-2-l Attaching the face frame

Figure 10-2-m Clamping the face frame to the cabinet body

Figure 10-2-n Applying edge banding

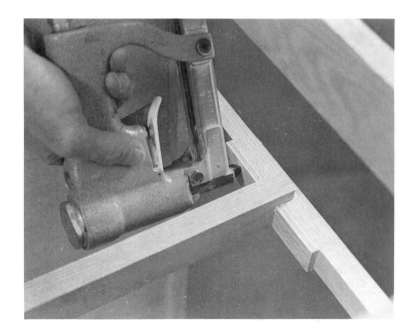

Figure 10-2-o Attaching drawer guides

Figure 10-2-p Attaching plastic guide tabs

Figure 10-2-q Attaching the tip rail

Figure 10-2-r Filling nail holes

for a few minutes as shown in Figure 10-2m. It is very important that the joint be very tight, since it will be highly visible.

The edge banding is now applied to the front edges of the cabinet bottom and shelves (Figure 10-2n). This edge banding is 3/8 in. thick if lip doors are to be used and 3/4 in. thick for overlay doors.

If center drawer guides are used, they may be attached now (Figure 10-2o). See Chapter 8 for details on drawer guides.

The plastic guide tabs are attached to the face frame on either side of the drawer opening (Figure 10-2p).

The tip rail for top drawers is attached next (Figure 10-2q).

All nail holes are then filled with a wood filler (Figure 10-2r).

Figure 10-3 Belt-sanding the face frame

SANDING THE CABINET

The cabinet is then sanded. A portable belt sander may be used for the preliminary sanding and to level face-frame joints if the face frame was not previously sanded with a wide-belt sander (Figure 10-3). Great care must be exercised when using the portable belt sander. It is very easy to dig gouges into the wood if it is not held perfectly flat. All cross-grain scratches should be removed with the belt sander.

The face-frame-to-cabinet joint should be carefully sanded (Figure 10-4). Be careful not to sand through the plywood veneer. The cabinet is then completely sanded with a finish sander (Figure 10-5). All sharp edges should be slightly eased with a sanding block (Figure 10-6).

Figure 10-4 Sanding the face-frame joint on the cabinet finished end

Figure 10-5 Final sanding with a finish sander

Figure 10-6 Easing sharp edges with a sanding block

INSTALLING DRAWERS

Drawers are installed by sliding the drawer into the opening while supporting the drawer guide (Figure 10-7). When the rear of the drawer guide is positioned for best drawer fit, an assistant can drive a staple or nail through the back of the cabinet into the guide. This may be later reinforced with wood screws.

Figure 10-7 Fitting the drawer

HANGING DOORS

The doors are mounted with the cabinet lying on its back on the bench. First, the hinges are mounted on the doors (Figure 10-8). Next, the doors are set in the proper opening in the cabinet and lined up flush with the bottom of the cabinet (Figure 10-9).

The doors are then attached to the cabinet (Figure 10-10).

The operation of hanging doors may vary with different types of hinges and doors. The hinge manufacturer's directions should be followed.

If roll-out trays are to be installed, they may be done now. The roller guide track is often mounted on the cabinet partitions before the cabinet is assembled.

ASSEMBLING THE WALL CABINET

The series of photographs in Figure 10-11 shows the assembly of a wall cabinet. Following this sequence, the nail holes are filled, the cabinet is sanded, and the doors are hung, just as on the base cabinet. The doors are sometimes left off wall cabinets until they have been installed to make it easier to lift the cabinet into place.

Figure 10-8-a&b Mounting hinges on the door. Notice the hinge jig used to mark the location of the screw holes.

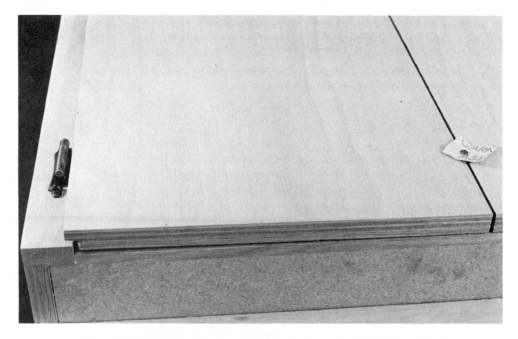

Figure 10-9 Positioning the doors in the cabinet opening. Notice the nails used as spacers between the pair of doors.

Figure 10-10 Attaching the doors to the cabinet.

Figure 10-11-a Installing an adjustable shelf standard. The adjustable shelf standards are installed before the cabinet is assembled. These must be numbered in groups of four for each opening and must be installed with the numbers reading right side up. They may be installed with special nails or with staples, using a stapler made for this purpose as shown here.

Figure 10-11-b The ends are then attached.

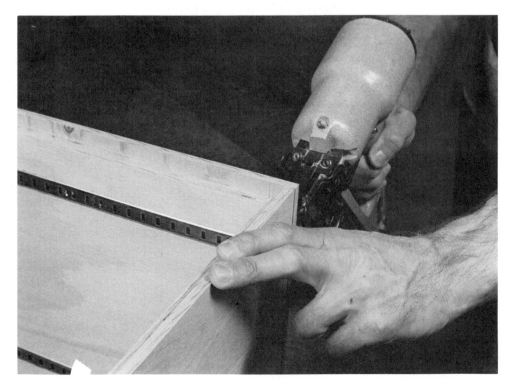

Figure 10-11-c The nailing strip is attached.

Figure 10-11-d The back is attached and used to square the cabinet, as on the base cabinet.

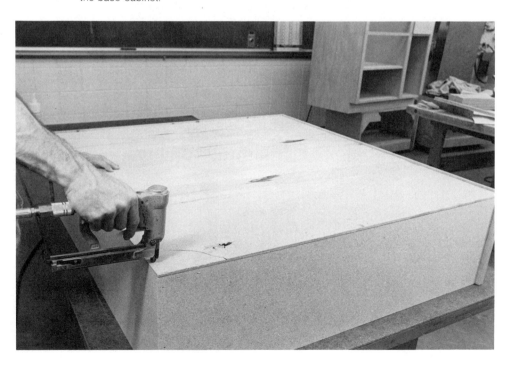

Figure 10-11-e The cabinet is turned over, and the face frame and edge banding are attached.

Figure 10-11-f Adjustable shelves are edge-banded and nail holes are filled and sanded. Notice the V block used to hold them in position for edge banding and sanding.

Chapter 11

Finishing

Finishing can be one of the most satisfying and one of the most frustrating operations in cabinetmaking—satisfying because it suddenly and dramatically changes the cabinets from the raw-wood state to that of fine furniture, if properly done, and frustrating because there are so many things that can go wrong.

Let's look at some of the problem areas first. Many finishing products are highly flammable, so strict regulations must be observed in storing and using finishes. Local regulations may affect the type of storage cabinet that may be used for storing finishes and the quantity of finishes that may be stored. Special explosionproof electrical fixtures are usually required in finishing areas, and special rag containers may be required.

Many finishes give off harmful vapors and fumes, so special exhaust ventilation requirements must also be met.

Some finishes have very slow drying times that may slow production. There are many finishing products on the market, some of which are not compatible with others.

The finishing area must be clean and free of dust for best results.

In this chapter we look at some of the more popular cabinet-finishing materials and methods.

PREPARING THE WOOD FOR FINISHING

The old saying that "a finish is no better than the surface it is applied to" is very true in wood finishing. A good wood finish will not hide sanding scratches, glue spots, mill marks, and the like. In fact, it will probably emphasize these defects.

Any excess glue must be carefully cut from the surface with a sharp chisel or knife. Small surface dents in the wood may be removed by placing a drop of water in the dent and letting it swell the fibers to raise the dent. For layer dents, steam may be used. A wet rag is placed on the dent, and a heat source such as a soldering pencil or clothes iron is placed on the rag over the dent. The steam usually swells the compressed wood and brings it back to its original level. If the wood fibers are cut or badly crushed, a wood filler is used. The filler should be checked to be sure that it will accept a stain if one is to be applied.

Another method of filling defects involves using a lacquer stick selected to match the final finish color. The lacquer stick melts with heat and then solidifies as it cools. A knife blade is heated and used to melt a small quantity of the lacquer stick. This material is then quickly pressed into the hole to be filled (Figure 11-1). Lacquer sticks make a very firm, permanent repair.

Figure 11-1 Using a lacquer stick to repair a hole in the wood

Once the glue has been removed and all repairs made, the sanding may be completed as described in Chapter 10. For most cabinetwork, the final sanding is completed with 120- to 180-grit paper. If an orbital sander is used, a finish hand sanding should follow to remove any swirl marks left by the orbital sander.

The surface should then be cleaned of dust by brushing or blowing with compressed air and then wiping with a tack rag.

FINISHING PRODUCTS

Most finishing products used in cabinet finishing fit into one of the following categories: presealers, stains, woodgrain fillers, sealers, surface top coats, and penetrating finishes. We will look briefly at each category and its place in the finishing process. It should be noted that not all finishing schedules require application of a product from each category.

Presealers: These products are sometimes applied to the raw wood before staining. They seal the wood partially to control the staining action of the stain. They are especially useful when there is a substantial amount of end grain or wavy, uneven grain, which tends to accept stain unevenly. Generally, a wood that has been presealed will accept slightly less stain (will not stain as dark) but will stain more evenly or uniformly.

Stains: There are several types of stain available for cabinetmaking. These include water stains, oil stains, non-grain-raising (NGR) stains, and chemical stains.

Water stains have some important advantages. They are generally considered to give the clearest, most transparent, and most permanent color of any stain. They resist fading when exposed to sunlight. They do not bleed into subsequent finish coats, and they are relatively inexpensive since they are purchased as a water-soluble powder and then mixed with hot water.

Unfortunately, they have two disadvantagaes that limit their use in production cabinetmaking. Their water base tends to raise the wood grain, so the wood must be sponged or predampened, allowed to dry, and resanded before the stain is applied. They also dry rather slowly for production work. They may be brushed on, but spraying is the best application method because it eliminates overlap marks from brushing. Water stains are not useful in refinishing wood because they will not penetrate a previously sealed surface.

Oil stains may be classified as one of two types, depending on the type of coloring agent used. Penetrating oil stains use an oil-soluble dye to color the wood, whereas pigmented oil stains (also known as wiping stains) use pigmented colors ground in the oil.

The penetrating stain will give greater clarity, since there is no pigment to obscure the woodgrain. The pigment stains are somewhat easier to use, as it is easy to wipe excess pigment from the surface to control the color of the wood.

Oil stains are generally easier to use than other stains, especially if they must be brushed or wiped on. They do not raise the woodgrain.

Their main disadvantages are that their color is not as permanent as water stains, so they will fade with exposure to light. Oil stains must be thoroughly dry before applying top coats because they have a tendency to bleed into the top coat. They may require as much as 24 hr. drying time. They may also affect the ability of certain top coats to bond to the surface. The manufacturer's directions should be followed carefully.

In spite of these disadvantages, oil stains remain popular, especially for small shops not involved in a large volume of finishing work.

Non-grain-raising (NGR) stains were developed in an effort to obtain the clarity and permanence of water stains without the undesirable side effect of grain raising. The results were largely successful, and these stains are often used in production woodworking. They use a soluble dye as do water stains, but instead of water they use solvents such as alcohol, toluol, glycol, and certain ketones. They dry very fast with moderate penetration and usually must be sprayed. For this reason they have found limited acceptance for general use by amateur woodworkers but are popular in production shops.

Chemical stains are rarely used in production cabinetmaking because of the time involved. However, it is possible on certain woods to obtain some interesting colors that are impossible to duplicate with conventional stains. Chemical stains do not stain the wood with dyes or pigments as conventional stains do; the color of the wood is changed by a chemical reaction between the chemical being used and substances in the wood.

Fumed oak is one of the best-known chemical staining processes. In this process, the wood to be stained is placed in an airtight tent with an open container of highly concentrated ammonia. The gas evaporating from the ammonia reacts with acids in the oak to change the color of the wood. A different color may be obtained by brushing the liquid ammonia directly on the wood surface.

Chemicals such as copper sulfate, iron sulfate, lime, acetic acid, potassium dichromate, and others may be used to impart different colors to certain woods.

There are a number of other products on the market designed to impart color to wood. Some of these combine stain with another finishing product such as filler, varnish, or lacquer in an effort to eliminate one or more steps from the finishing schedule. Most of these result in serious compromises in the quality or appearance of the finish and are not generally recommended for quality work. Two exceptions would be toning lacquer and penetrating oil finishes with stains.

Toning lacquer is a lacquer with a compatible coloring agent used to give a transparent colored film. It should not be used in place of staining; if it is, all the color will be on top of the surface and the slightest scratch would show the original color of the wood. It is, however, often used to bring cabinets or furniture to a more uniform color after the initial staining. It may also be used to highlight certain areas.

Penetrating oil finishes (discussed later in this chapter) such as Danish oil and tung oil work very well when combined with a stain and are available in various wood colors.

Woodgrain Fillers: Open-grain woods such as oak, Philippine mahogany, and ash are sometimes filled to provide a smooth surface for applying the finish top coats. This is a very slow process, and while it is often done in furniture construction, its use in cabinetmaking is usually limited to the very finest work.

This filler is a thin paste available in standard stain colors that is applied to the surface with a rag in a circular motion that packs it into the wood pores. It is then allowed to dry to a dull finish (usually 10 to 20 min.); then the excess material is removed from the surface by wiping across the grain with burlap or some other coarse cloth. A final light wiping, in the direction of the grain, is done with a soft cloth, and the surface is allowed to dry thoroughly before the next finishing product is applied.

Sealers: Some top-coat finishes require that a sealer be used before the top coats are applied; others do not. The manufacturer's recommendations should be followed. Lacquer finishes, for example, are usually preceded by one coat of lacquer sanding sealer. This sealer is designed to adhere well to the surface, providing a good bond between the lacquer and the wood surface. It also sands easily to allow removal of any roughness before the final coats are applied. Varnish sealers and shellac sealers are also available.

Surface Top Coats: Top-coat finishes used for cabinets include oleoresinous varnishes, polyurethanes, lacquers, and shellacs. The vast majority of cabinets built in small to medium-sized shops are finished with lacquer of some type.

There are several good reasons for the popularity of lacquer as a cabinet finish. One of the most compelling reasons for using lacquer in a production situation is its rapid drying time. Many lacquers are dry to the touch in 5 min. and can be recoated in as little as 30 min. In addition to the obvious advantage of speeding production, this decreases the likelihood of airborne dust settling on the wet surface as it is prone to do on a finish that remains wet for several hours.

Lacquers are very durable and resistant to most common household liquids. They also give the wood a very attractive luster without having a thick buildup look, and they are easier to touch up than other clear finishes.

Hot lacquer and catalyzed lacquers are sometimes employed in situations where a shop does enough finishing work to warrant the extra investment in equipment.

The hot-lacquer process uses a lacquer similar to conventional spraying lacquer that is heated to 140° to 160° F and sprayed at that temperature. The major advantage of this process is that the heat reduces the viscosity of the lacquer, so a lacquer with a higher solids content may be sprayed. (The solids content of a lacquer determines the thickness of the film left on the wood after the solvents and thinners have evaporated. A lacquer for spraying at room temperature may have 21% solids, while a lacquer for hot spraying may have 35% solids.) Therefore, it is often possible to obtain a film thickness with one coat of hot lacquer that would require two coats of cold lacquer.

Catalyzed lacquers have the advantage of increasing the hardness and toughness of the lacquer film and of speeding the drying process. Even though conventional lacquer dries to the touch very rapidly, it remains fairly soft and sensitive to damage for several days. Catalyzed lacquers harden much faster, making it safe to handle or ship finished items sooner after finishing. The lacquer and catalyst must be mixed and then used within a specified time, ranging from a few hours to several weeks.

Lacquers are not without their disadvantages. They are very difficult to brush because they dry so rapidly. Lacquers and their thinners are highly flammable, so they must be carefully stored. Since they are usually sprayed, an exhaust system is required to maintain proper ventilation. They are generally not good for exterior finishing.

Oleoresinous varnishes are not used a great deal in commercial cabinet finishing because of their slow drying time. However, they do provide an excellent finish where speed is not important, especially when spray equipment is not available.

Polyurethane finishes evolved from varnishes, with synthetic materials replacing the natural resins and oils found in oleoresinous varnishes. The polyurethane finishes are extremely hard and tough and will not yellow with age as a varnish finish will. They are somewhat more difficult to apply smoothly than the best varnish finishes, and their use is somewhat limited in cabinet finishing, again, because of drying-time considerations.

Shellac is one of the oldest clear wood finishes and is still an excellent product for certain situations. It is still the best clear sealer to use over oily or resinous surfaces such as those often encountered when working with pine. This, in fact, is its major application in cabinetmaking. It has a short shelf life and will not dry properly when it is too old. Any shellac over a year old is suspect and should be applied to a test piece of scrap wood to check for drying.

It may be necessary, after the final top coat, to remove the slight irregularities left by brushing or spraying and to improve the final luster. This can be accomplished by buffing the surface with a very fine steel wool (000 or 0000) and paste wax. The steel-wool pad is dipped in the paste wax and the surface is buffed to remove any high spot or roughness and to apply a coat of wax. The wax is allowed to dry and is then buffed with a soft cloth.

To obtain a very fine, mirror-smooth furniture finish, a more elaborate rub-out procedure is used. The final top coat is allowed to dry thoroughly (several days for lacquer, several weeks for varnish) and is sanded with 600-grit wet-or-dry paper, using water as a lubricant. This levels any high spots. The sanding scratches are then polished out using pumice first, then rottenstone. The pumice is a fine powdered abrasive that is mixed with mineral oil to make a paste. It is applied with a felt pad or a pad made by folding a cotton cloth. The surface is rubbed briskly to polish out the scratches. The rottenstone, which is an even finer abrasive, is used in the same way. When properly done, this results in a mirror-smooth surface, and a coat of lemon-oil polish can be applied. Obviously, this is a very time-consuming operation and is usually used on only the finest work.

Penetrating Oil Finishes: The surface finishes discussed up to this point protect the wood by forming a hard film on its surface. Penetrating oil finishes, on the other hand, penetrate into the wood and harden in the wood through a polymerization process. Danish oil and tung oil are two such products. They both give excellent results and are easy to apply without any special equipment. Many people also prefer the more natural appearance of oiled wood to that finished with a surface finish.

The application procedure varies with different products and different manufacturers, but it generally consists of wiping oil on the surface, keeping the surface wet with oil for a specified time, and then wiping the surface dry. Sometimes the first coat is wet-sanded into the wood. The process is usually repeated several times at 12- to 24-hr. intervals. With most woods, it takes several applications to achieve a rich sheen. A final protective coat of wax may be applied.

One word of caution: *Rags saturated with Danish oil or tung oil are prone to spontaneous combustion. They should never be left lying around or put in garbage cans after finishing. They should be soaked in water and disposed of promptly.*

FINISHING EQUIPMENT

The most widely used finish for general cabinetmaking is lacquer, which is almost always applied by spraying. Therefore, we will concentrate our discussion of finishing equipment on spray finishing equipment. However, since brushes are sometimes used for small jobs, we will also look briefly at that method of application.

It is possible to obtain a good-quality finish using the proper product and a good-quality brush. However, a good-quality finish is not likely to result from using a 49¢ brush from a dime store. The type of bristle is the major factor in determining the quality of the brush. Ideally, each individual bristle is tapered (thicker at the shank end), oval in cross section, and split or flagged at the small end. The only animal considerate enough to provide such a bristle is a certain wild Chinese hog. Consequently, good Chinese bristle brushes are very expensive. Good-quality nylon-bristle brushes have been developed with most of the same qualities and are less expensive and longer-lasting. There are many other types of brushes using natural (animal hair) or artificial bristles, but unless the bristles are tapered, flagged, and oval in cross section, they will not have a good brushing action and will have a limited capacity for holding finish. The tapered bristle gives a good spring action to the brush by allowing it to flex near the tip and remain stiff near the shank. The flagged end helps it carry a large amount of finish, and the oval cross section helps keep the bristles from becoming tangled.

Various finishes require different brushing techniques, so the manufacturer's instructions should be followed.

Spray finishing (using conventional air spraying) requires the following equipment: an air compressor, a pressure regulator, and a moisture extractor. The regulator and extractor are often combined as one unit. The air compressor is made up of the compressor unit (air pump), a motor, and a storage tank. It is usually equipped with a pressure switch to turn the motor off when the air pressure reaches a predetermined level and to start it when the pressure drops to a cerain point. Compressors are generally rated according to their air output in cubic feet per minute (cfm) at certain pressures. A small portable compressor might put out 7 cfm at a pressure of 40 lb. per square inch (psi), while a larger stationary compressor might put out 40 cfm at 40 psi. To determine the size of compressor needed, it is necessary to determine the cfm requirement of the tools that the compressor is to operate. Some production spray guns require 10 to 12 cfm. Other air-powered equipment in the shop must also be considered. Many shops use air-powered nail and staple guns, sanders, clamps, drills, and routers.

The air-pressure regulator is used to deliver the proper air pressure to the gun for the material being sprayed. The line pressure (air pressure directly from the compressor) is often in excess of 100 psi. The air-pressure regulator reduces this to the necessary 35 to 40 psi for spraying lacquer.

The moisture extractor, as its name suggests, removes moisture and oil from the air line to provide clean, dry air to the spray gun. This is very important. When air is compressed it is heated, and when it cools in the line, water condensation results. If this water were allowed to go through the line to the gun and mix with the lacquer, it would spoil the finish.

The spray gun is the most important part of the system. It must provide nearly perfect atomization of the finish and must spray in a consistent, uniform pattern. The gun should have an adjustment to change the shape of the spray pattern and an adjustment to control volume.

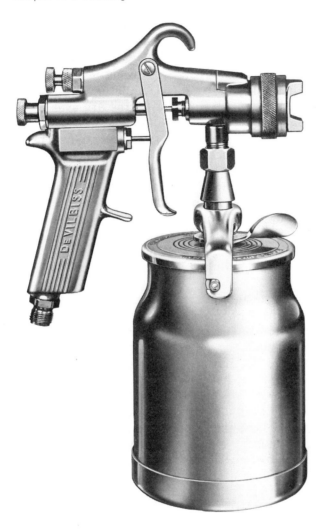

Figure 11-2 A suction-feed spray gun. (Courtesy of the DeVilbiss Co.)

Spray guns can be classified as suction-feed or pressure-feed. The suction-feed gun has the finish container attached to the gun and is usually limited to about 1 qt. capacity. The air cap is designed so that the air moving through the gun creates a low-pressure area that draws the liquid from the cup up the pickup tube to the spray head (Figure 11-2).

Suction-feed guns are not often used for production spraying because their limited capacity requires frequent refilling and the extra weight of the quart of finish in the cup is fatiguing to the operator. They are an excellent choice, though, for small shops that occasionally finish cabinets. They are easy to set up and easy to clean.

Pressure-feed guns use air pressure to force the material through the gun. They may have a pressurized paint cup on the gun, but more often they will have a remote paint pot connected to the gun by a fluid line. The operator has to contend only with the weight of the gun and does not have to refill as frequently, since the paint pot may hold 5 gal. or more of finish.

Spray guns may be further classified as external-mix or internal-mix, depending on whether air and fluid are mixed (fluid atomization) just outside the air cap or inside the air cap. External-mix caps are usually used with fast-drying finishes such as lacquers.

Airless spraying, which uses hydraulic pressure rather than compressed air to atomize the paint, is becoming increasingly popular in production cabinet shops. A high-pressure pump replaces the air compressor in this system, and the liquid finish is atomized by being forced through an accurately shaped orifice at very high pressure, usually over 2,000 psi.

Airless spraying has several advantages over conventional air spraying. There is less overspray than when the liquid is atomized with air. It is much easier to spray inside the cabinets and into corners because the "bounceback" that occurs with air spraying is eliminated. Higher-viscosity fluids may also be sprayed.

Electrostatic spraying is yet another finishing process that is being used by some large production shops. This process has been in use for a number of years for finishing metal items. The item to be finished is given a positive electrical charge (often through the conveyor system that moves the items through the finish area), and the finish is given a negative charge (a negative electrode in the gun). Since unlike charges attract, the negatively charged paint particles are attracted to the positively charged item. Wood items are pretreated with an electrolytic solution so that they can be given a positive charge. The finish may even be applied by being fed by hose to the center of a revolving disk. The disk, which has a negative charge, rotates rapidly, and the finish moves across the disk by centrifugal force and is atomized as it is thrown off the edge of the disk.

Electrostatic finishing offers the following advantages:

1.   The finish tends to build at a uniform thickness.
2.   There is little wasted material and little overspray because all the finish is attracted to the article being finished.
3.   It lends itself well to automation when many similar items are to be finished.

SPRAY FINISHING TECHNIQUES

Conventional air-spray finishing involves several variables, each of which can cause problems with the finish. The air pressure must be correct for the material being sprayed. The gun must be aimed perpendicular to the surface, must be at the correct distance from the surface, must be moved at the correct speed, and must be adjusted properly.

The series of photographs in Figure 11-3 shows the procedure for spraying lacquer on a cabinet end. First, adjust the gun to get a fan- or oval-shaped pattern (Figure 11-3a). Hold the gun perpendicular to the surface at a distance of about 6 in. (Figure 11-3b). Whenever possible, start the gun *off* the surface to be sprayed (Figure 11-3c). Move it across the surface being sprayed, and stop after moving it past the other edge of the surface. This will avoid the possibility of starting the spray before moving the gun and getting a thick buildup in that spot.

For the second pass, the gun is aimed at the bottom edge of the wet finish from the first pass. This allows each pass to overlap the previous area and prevents thin areas of finish that would normally occur at the edge of the spray pattern (Figure 11-3d).

This process is repeated until the end of the cabinet is covered. The gun is started off the edge of the cabinet, moved across the cabinet, and stopped on the other side, dropped one half pattern width, started, and moved back across the cabinet.

Figure 11-3-a Adjusting the spray gun

Figure 11-3-b The spray gun is held approximately 6 in. from the surface and perpendicular to it.

Figure 11-3-c Start the spray *off* the surface.

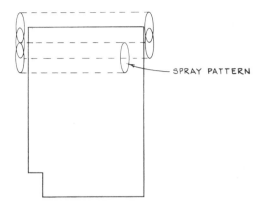

SPRAY PATTERN

Figure 11-3-d Overlapping the spray pattern

Figure 11-3-e It is *not* a good practice to spray diagonally into the corner of a cabinet.

The gun must be moved slowly enough to apply a wet film of lacquer, but not so slowly that the lacquer film gets thick and runs. If the gun is moved too rapidly or is held too far from the surface, a rough, powdery surface will result.

The inside surfaces of the cabinet are sprayed in much the same way. Keep the gun perpendicular to each surface. Do not spray diagonally into corners.

Figure 11-3-f Spraying the face frame

The air from the gun will bounce back and prevent the atomized finish from reaching the surface (Figure 11-3e). Reducing the air pressure sometimes makes it easier to spray inside cabinets. Make sure that the finish is being completely atomized, however.

The face frame is difficult to spray (Figure 11-3f) because it is easy to get a double wet coat where stiles and rails intersect. Some finishers prefer to spray the vertical stiles first and then spray all the horizontal rails, being careful not to respray the still-wet stiles.

All hardware is removed from doors and drawers before they are finished. They are sprayed by propping them in a convenient position in the spray booth and then removing them to a drying area to dry.

SUMMARY

While there are many finishing materials and processes suitable for finishing cabinets, the finishing schedule most often used by small to medium-sized cabinet shops would probably be something like the following:

1. The finish sanding is completed and all hardware is removed.
2. All dust is removed by vacuuming or blowing with compressed air and then wiping with a tack rag.
3. The cabinet is stained to the customer's preference.
4. After the stain is dry, the cabinet is sprayed with one coat of lacquer sanding sealer.
5. The lacquer sealer is lightly sanded, and the cabinet is sprayed with two coats of clear lacquer.

Chapter 12

Cabinet Installation

The cabinet shop may or may not be responsible for installing the cabinets. When the shop acts as a subcontractor in building cabinets for a general contractor, the cabinet shop is usually responsible for delivering the cabinets to the job site, where the general contractor installs them.

When the cabinet shop does work for a private customer, especially on remodel work, the shop is usually also responsible for installation of the cabinets. Shops that do a lot of installation work sometimes have a special crew just for that purpose. Even if a cabinetmaker never installs cabinets, it is good to have a knowledge of the installation process because there are many little things that can be done to make it easier for the person installing the cabinets.

Some cabinetmakers install the wall cabinets first so that they don't have to work around the base cabinets. They use long jack stands to hold each cabinet in place until it is fitted and nailed in place. Others prefer setting the base cabinets first, putting the countertop substrate on, and then using short jack stands on the base cabinet to support the wall cabinet. This is the method that is described in this chapter.

SETTING BASE CABINETS

A set of kitchen base cabinets is made up of a number of smaller units. Before the installation begins, the best sequence for installing the units should be determined. If there is a corner cabinet, such as a Lazy Susan cabinet, it is often best to start with that and then attach the other cabinets to it. If the floor is not level, as is sometimes the case in an older house where settling may have occurred, it is usually necessary to start at the high point of the floor. This will allow adjacent cabinets to be shimmed to keep the countertop level.

The series of photographs in Figure 12-1 illustrates the cabinet-installation process. First, set the cabinet in place and check to see that it is setting level (Figure 12-1a). The cabinet should be checked for level along its length by setting the level on the face frame, and it should be checked for level from front to back. If it is not level, slip shim shingles (narrow wood shingles) under the cabinet to level it.

The alignment of door pairs should be checked at this point also. Assuming that the cabinet was on a flat, level surface when the doors were hung, they should hang level when the cabinet is setting level. The doors in Figure 12-1b indicate that the cabinet needs to be raised on the right side to make the doors level with each other.

When the cabinet is level, it is ready to be scribed or fitted to the wall. A scribing tool is used to mark the contour of the wall on the edge of the face frame (Figures 12-1c and 12-1d). The same thing is done when a finished end joins the wall (Figure 12-1e).

The cabinet is then pulled back from the wall, and a block plane or small power plane is used to plane to the scribe line (Figure 12-1f). This allows the

Figure 12-1-a Checking to see that the cabinet is setting level

Figure 12-1-b Cabinet doors
not level

Figure 12-1-c Scribing tool

Figure 12-1-d Scribing the face frame to the wall

Figure 12-1-e Scribing a finished end to the wall

Figure 12-1-f Planing to the scribe line

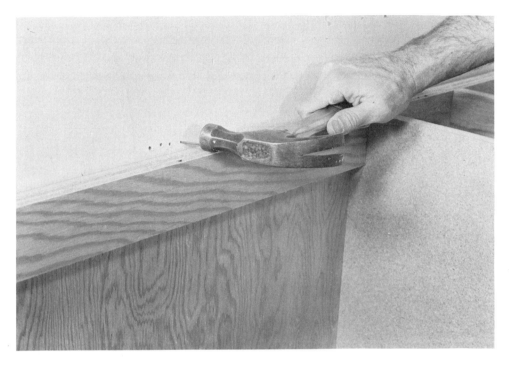

Figure 12-1-g Locating wall studs

cabinet to be fitted very tightly against the wall despite any minor irregularities in the wall surface. It eliminates the need to use a molding to cover gaps that would otherwise occur between the cabinet and the wall.

The cabinet is then pushed back against the wall, releveled, and checked for fit.

If everything fits properly, the wall studs are located and the cabinet is nailed in place with 16d nails. The wall studs may be located (Figure 12-1g) by tapping on the wallboard to get an approximate location by sound and then driving a small nail through the wallboard to determine the exact location. The nail should be driven through the wallboard just above the cabinet in the area that will eventually be covered by the countertop and backsplash. When a stud is located, its exact center should be determined be making a series of small holes. From the center of this stud, the others can usually be located by measuring 16 in. intervals.

The cabinet is permanently attached by nailing through the nailing strip on the back of the cabinet into the wall studs. If the back of the cabinet is not tight against the wall (it may be held out by the back scribe on a finished end), a shim shingle should be inserted behind the cabinet at each nailing location to prevent bowing the back of the cabinet (Figure 12-1h). The wall end of the cabinet may be nailed to the wall in the same way (Figure 12-1i).

Figure 12-1-h It may be necessary to use shim shingles when the back is nailed to the wall.

Figure 12-1-i Nailing the wall end

Figure 12-2 Rough plumbing for a sink

Adjacent cabinets are then usually bolted together. After the first cabinet has been set, the one adjacent to it is leveled, bolted to the first one, and nailed to the wall.

When the plans call for a range, dishwasher, or other appliance, it is very important that the cabinets be set so as to allow adequate room for the appliance. The actual width of the appliance should be checked. A 30-in. range, for example, usually requires a 30 1/2-in. opening between cabinets.

A sink cabinet must have holes drilled in the back (or occasionally the bottom) of the cabinet to allow for the plumbing. In new construction, the three pipes (hot water, cold water, and drain) extend through the wall about 6 in. and are capped (Figure 12-2). Accurate measurements are taken to determine where the pipes will go through the cabinet, and holes are drilled through the cabinet back (Figure 12-3). When an auger bit is used, the hole should be started from the back until the lead screw breaks through the cabinet back. Then the hole should be finished from inside the cabinet to avoid splintering. The cabinet is slipped into place and nailed. The plumbers will complete the plumbing after the countertop is installed and the sink can be set in place.

When the base cabinets are all in place, the countertop substrate (usually 3/4-in. industrial particle board) can be set in place and nailed down (Figure 12-4). It usually extends 1/4 in. beyond the front of the cabinet. If the

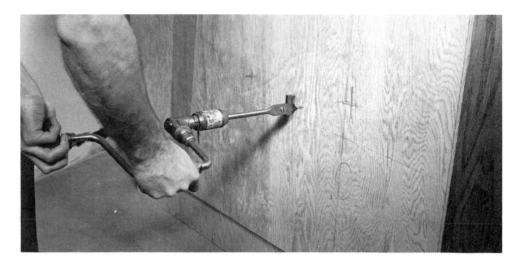

Figure 12-3 Drilling through the cabinet back for plumbing

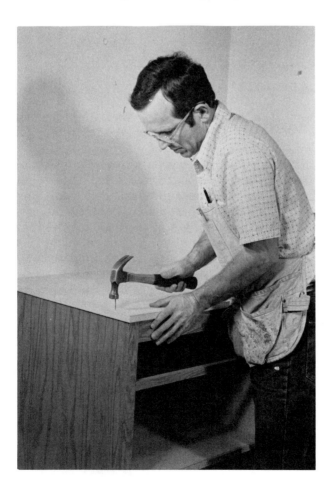

Figure 12-4 Installing particle board for the countertop

Figure 12-5 Installing the countertop edge strip

countertop is to be covered with plastic laminate and is to have a plastic laminate edge band, the edging strip is also applied (Figure 12-5).

SETTING WALL CABINETS

Before putting the wall cabinets in place, the distance between the countertop and the bottom of the wall cabinet should be determined. A pair of simple wood jack stands are then built to support the wall cabinet at the proper height while it is being nailed in place (Figure 12-6). It is usually best to remove the doors from wall cabinets before installing them. If the cabinet is to fit against the ceiling, the jack stand should be 1/2 in. lower to allow the cabinet to be lifted into place. Shim shingles are then used to shim it tightly against the ceiling.

After the cabinet has been lifted onto the jack stands, the procedure for leveling and scribing it to the wall is similar to that used for base cabinets.

When the cabinet is taken back down to plane the scribe, the wall studs must be located. Their location from the end wall must be measured and noted. Their location must then be marked inside the cabinet, measuring from the wall end of the cabinet (Figure 12-7). Be sure to allow for the thickness of the end and wall scribe, if any.

Figure 12-6 Jack stands for supporting wall cabinets

Figure 12-7 Marking stud location inside a cabinet

After the scribe has been planed and stud locations marked, the cabinet is set back up on the jack stands, checked, and nailed into place. Large cabinets and those that will carry heavy loads should also be attached with lag screws.

One of the more difficult cabinet-installation situations is the installation of a cabinet that must fit between two walls. If the cabinet can be made smaller than the opening and the resulting gap covered with a molding, there is no problem, but it is very difficult to fit the cabinet tightly to the two walls. If this is necessary, it is best to leave the face frame off the cabinet until the cabinet has been nailed in place. The face frame is first planed until it fits the opening and is then nailed to the cabinet.

FINAL CHECK

After the cabinets are installed, a final check should be made to be sure that everything is properly adjusted and working. It is less expensive (and less embarrassing!) to make sure that everything is right before leaving the job rather than being called back by the owner. The doors should be checked to be sure that they lie flat against the face of the cabinet when closed. If they touch the cabinet at one corner but not the other, it indicates that either the cabinet is twisted or the door is warped. If the problem is severe, its source should be found and corrected. If it is slight, there are several adjustments that can be made. If double demountable hinges are used, one hinge (the one diagonally opposite the high corner of the door) is adjusted outward. This can be accomplished with some other types of hinges by bending the hinge slightly. Some hinge manufacturers even provide a special tool for this purpose. Another alternative is to loosen the screws that hold the hinge to the door and slip a thin cardboard shim under the hinge. This moves that corner of the door away from the face of the cabinet and moves the diagonally opposite corner closer to the cabinet face.

The gap between pairs of doors should be uniform, about 1/16 in.

Door and drawer pulls or knobs should be installed, and any nail holes that were not previously filled should be filled. If the cabinets were prefinished before installation, any unfilled nail holes may be filled with a soft wax filler. These fillers are available in jars or in stick form in a wide variety of colors to match almost any finish.

Finally, the site should be cleaned up. Your completed job will look better in a clean environment. Besides, the floor covering people wouldn't appreciate having to remove the wood shavings, bent nails, and hinge packages you left before they can go to work!

Chapter 13

Installing Plastic Laminate Countertops

Plastic laminate countertops are sometimes installed by the cabinetmaker. The plastic laminate parts are usually cut slightly oversize in the shop and then taken to the job site for installation. Plastic laminates can be cut with most woodworking tools, but carbide cutters are recommended because ordinary high-speed steel cutters will dull quickly when used for cutting plastic laminates.

CUTTING PARTS TO SIZE

The laminate sheets are usually cut to rough countertop size on the table saw. The top should be cut 1/4 in. to 1/2 in. oversize to allow for trimming to size. A fine-toothed carbide plywood blade works well, although special blades are available for this purpose. When cutting plastic laminates on the table saw, the rip fence must be checked to be sure that there is not a gap between the bottom of the fence and the table surface that would allow the laminate sheet to slide under the fence (Figure 13-1). It may be necessary to clamp a wood facing board to the fence to eliminate the gap.

Figure 13-2 shows a sheet of laminate being cut to size.

If the countertop is to have a plastic laminate edge band, this is also cut at this time. The edge band is usually cut 1/8 in. oversize, so a 1 1/4-in. edge band would be cut 1 3/8 in. wide. The plastic laminate backsplash parts are also cut, and the parts are taken to the job site for installation.

Figure 13-1 Checking the rip fence to make sure that the thin plastic laminate sheet will not slip under the fence while it is being cut

Figure 13-2 Cutting a laminate sheet to size

The surface on which the laminate is applied must be clean and flat. A small wood chip or other foreign object will leave a noticeable bump on the finished surface.

APPLYING THE EDGE BAND

If the countertop is to have a plastic laminate edge band, this is applied first. A coat of contact cement is brushed on the edge of the countertop and on the plastic laminate edge-band strips. After the first coat on the countertop edge dries, a second one is applied to make sure that the porous wood surface is completely coated (Figure 13-3).

After the cement is dry to the touch (usually 15 to 20 min.), the edge banding is applied. The edge-band strip is started where a countertop joins a wall or at the end of the cabinet (Figure 13-4). The strip is held flush with the bottom edge of the countertop, leaving 1/8 in. overlap at the top for trimming. A bond is developed as soon as the edge banding touches the countertop, so care must be taken to start at one end and work along the edge, pressing the edge band against the countertop as you go. After the edge band is in place,

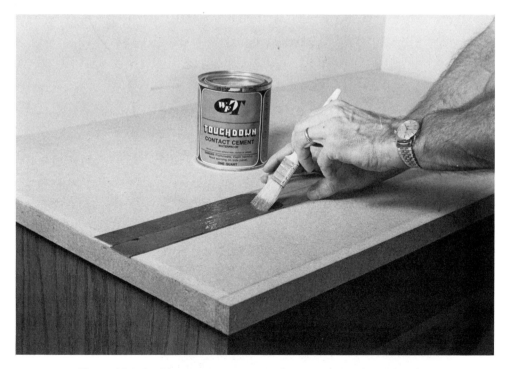

Figure 13-3 Applying contact cement to the countertop edge and to the plastic laminate edge band

Figure 13-4 Applying the edge band

Figure 13-5 Plastic laminate–trimming bit for a portable router

additional pressure must be applied by running a rubber-wheeled roller over it.

The top edge of the edge-band strip must now be trimmed flush with the top surface of the countertop. This may be accomplished with a portable router and a special laminate-trimming bit (Figure 13-5). This trimming bit has a ball bearing pilot that guides the cutter along the edge of the countertop (Figure 13-6). Special laminate-trimming routers are also available for this purpose.

After the edge band is trimmed, a belt sander is used to sand the top edge lightly to remove any excess contact cement and to make sure that it is flush with the countertop (Figure 13-7).

Figure 13-6 Using the router to trim the edge banding

Figure 13-7 The top edge is lightly belt-sanded.

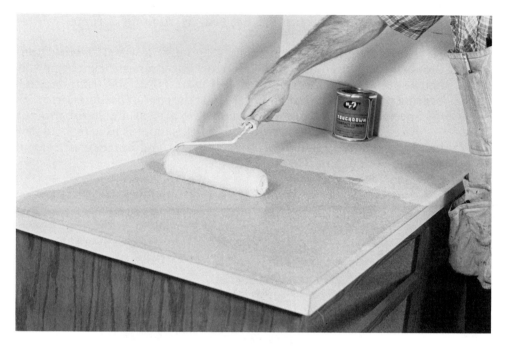

Figure 13-8 Applying contact cement with a paint roller

APPLYING THE TOP

Contact cement is usually applied to large surfaces, such as countertops, with a short-nap paint roller (Figure 13-8). The particle-board top is given a second coat and allowed to dry. It is very difficult to set a large sheet of laminate down on a countertop without its sagging and sticking to the countertop before you are ready. This problem can be avoided by setting a series of spacers (old Venetian-blind slats are ideal) on the countertop and then setting the cemented laminate sheet on these strips (Figure 13-9).

The laminate sheet may now be positioned so that it overhangs the countertop slightly. When it is in proper position, the Venetian-blind slat at one end is pulled from under the laminate sheet and that end of the sheet is pressed down against the top to bond it (Figure 13-10). The remaining blind slats are now removed one at a time, starting from the end that has been bonded. The laminate sheet is carefully pressed down as the slats are removed to avoid bulges. If Venetian-blind slats are not available, strips of plastic laminate or strips of wood may be used. The top is also rolled with a rubber roller to apply additional pressure.

The overhanging edge is trimmed with a router-cutter similar to the one used to trim the edge banding except that the one used for the top surface trims the edge at a bevel (Figures 13-11 and 13-12).

Figure 13-9 Using spacers to keep the laminate from touching the counter-top until it has been properly positioned

Figure 13-10 Removing the spacer from one end

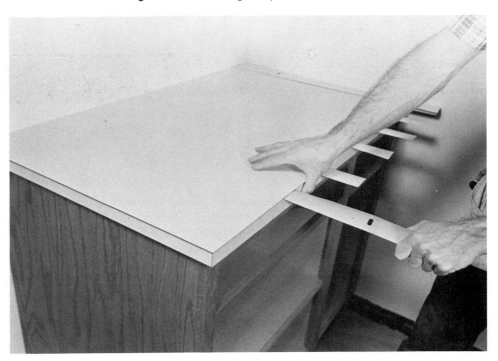

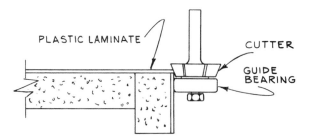

Figure 13-11 Router bit for trimming the edge of the laminate sheet flush with the edge of the counter

Figure 13-12 Using the bevel trimmer bit to trim the countertop

CUTOUT FOR A SINK

The hole for a sink is cut *before* the plastic laminate is applied. The particleboard countertop is marked for the sink location, and the sink cutout pattern is drawn on the surface and is cut out with a saber saw (Figure 13-13). The hole is covered by the plastic laminate sheet used on the countertop. The final cutout is made by drilling a hole in the sink cutout area large enough to insert the laminate-trimming router bit. The router is then started and moved toward one side of the sink cutout hole until the pilot bearing touches the edge of the hole. The router is then run around the perimeter of the hole to complete the cutout (Figure 13-14).

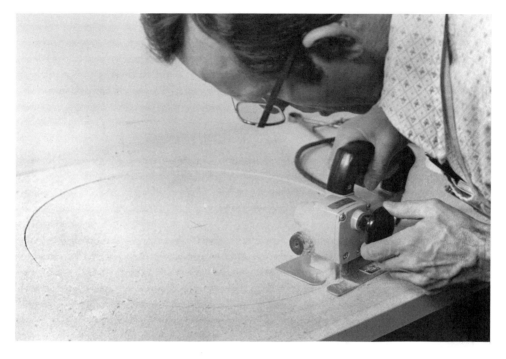

Figure 13-13 Making the sink cutout

Figure 13-14 Using the router to make the sink cutout in the plastic laminate

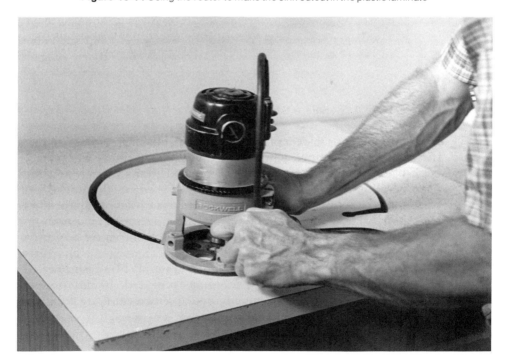

Figure 13-15 Aluminum back-splash molding

APPLYING THE BACKSPLASH

Many countertops have a plastic laminate backsplash applied to the wall along the back of the cabinet. This is usually 4 to 6 in. high. The plastic laminate backsplash is usually edged with an extruded aluminum molding made for this purpose. Figure 13-15 shows the molding used on the bottom edge of the backsplash to join it to the cabinet and the piece used to cap the top edge of the backsplash. These aluminum moldings must be cut to length and prefitted to the backsplash before it is installed. A simple wood miter box and a hacksaw (Figure 13-16) may be used to miter the corners, or a chop saw with an aluminum cutting blade may be used. Figure 13-17 shows a section of backsplash with the aluminum moldings prefitted. It may now be installed using a construction mastic cement applied with a caulking gun. It may also be installed with contact cement.

Figure 13-16 Wood miter box and hacksaw used to cut aluminum back-splash moldings

Figure 13-17 Backsplash moldings are cut and fitted prior to installation.

Figure 13-18 Final filing of the countertop edge

To complete the plastic laminate installation, all excess contact cement must be removed with a rag and lacquer thinner, and all edges must be filed smooth with a fine, single-cut file (Figure 13-18). Finally, the sharp edge of the countertop should be eased slightly with the file.

Chapter 14

Estimating and Bidding

Many cabinetmaking jobs are obtained by the bidding process—that is, a cabinet shop proposes to build a set of cabinets for a specified sum of money. A general contractor may invite several cabinet shops to submit bids for the cabinetwork for a building that the general contractor is bidding on. The general contractor will usually use the lowest cabinet bid in preparing the total bid. If he is successful in obtaining the job, he will then usually have the cabinet shop that submitted the lowest bid build the cabinets.

Private owners who are remodeling may also invite cabinet shops to submit bids. The owner is not obligated to accept the lowest bid. The owner may, in fact, prefer to have the work done by someone other than the low bidder and may negotiate with the shop to try to get the bid price reduced.

FACTORS INVOLVED IN PRICING CABINETWORK

At first glance, preparing a cabinetmaking bid would seem to be a simple operation. One merely determines the type, quantity, and price of materials needed and estimates the amount of time necessary to build the cabinets. However, there are many other costs that must be considered to determine what it actually costs to build cabinets. Cabinet shops usually have a substantial investment in equipment: saws, jointers, planers, shapers, and many other machines. These machines have a certain value when purchased. This value is reduced as they wear out or become obsolete. This is referred to as depreciation. For accounting and tax purposes, many machines are depreciated over a five-year period. A portion of this depreciation must be charged against each job.

Examples of other costs include rent or mortgage payments on the building, utilities (light, heat, power, water, sewer), various taxes, insurance, sharpening of cutting tools, equipment maintenance, janitorial service, interest payments, accounting services, office help, vehicle costs, procurement costs, supplies such as glue and sandpaper, and inventory costs. Labor costs must include not only the employees' hourly wages but also vacation pay, paid holidays, insurance, retirement, and all other benefits. This does not mean, however, that the cabinetmaker figures all of these costs, adds the desired profit, and prices the cabinets accordingly. Other cabinet shops are likely bidding on the same job, so your price must be lower or at least competitive with theirs if you are to have a chance to get the job. The person doing the bidding should be familiar with prices of other recent cabinetwork in the area.

The costs mentioned above are sometimes difficult to assign to a specific job, so rather than trying to determine how much electrical power was used on one job or how much equipment depreciation should be charged to a job, these overhead costs are averaged on an hourly basis. The average monthly expenses (not counting wages or material purchases) are totaled and divided by the number of working hours per month to get the average hourly cost of operating the shop. See Table 14-1 for a simple example of the expenses for a small shop.

Table 14-1 Average Monthly Expenses

Building rent	$ 500
Electricity (avg./mo.)	120
Heat (avg./mo.)	180
Equipment depreciation ($20,000 ÷ 60 mo.)	330
Insurance	100
Bookkeeper, secretary (half time)	700
Vehicle expenses	300
Taxes	100
Miscellaneous (phone, sharpening, etc.)	100
Owner's salary (owner does bidding, prepares shop drawings, etc.)	2,400
Average monthly expense	**$4,830**
	÷ 173
Average hourly costs	**$27.92**

In totaling the average monthly expenses, we find that the average total monthly expense is $4,830. Assuming that there are approximately 173 working hours per month, we find that it takes $27.92 per hour to cover the fixed costs of operating the shop. Fixed costs are those costs that remain essentially constant regardless of minor fluctuations in the volume of business. Administrative salaries are usually considered fixed costs.

SHOP TIME RATES

Now, let us assume that there are four cabinetmakers working in the shop and that their pay is $16 per hour, including all benefits. We have just found that it costs $27.92 per hour to operate the shop. If we divide that amount by four, we find that we must add $6.98 per hour to each employee's wages to get the true cost of doing business. This total cost per hour per employee would be $22.98. This figure is often the basis for calculating shop time rates. This figure may be increased somewhat to allow the company to build reserves for purchasing materials for future jobs and other anticipated expenses. If a shop has an especially expensive piece of equipment, the shop time rate may be increased on jobs using that equipment.

This figure can be used for estimating the labor when preparing a cabinet bid. This does not include a profit on the job. After the material costs and labor costs have been determined, the owner must add the profit to come up with the total bid price for the job. The profit may be 10% to 15% of the job price.

Two common methods are used to prepare estimates on cabinet prices. One method involves a detailed quantity takeoff to determine the quantity of materials, then determining the price of the materials, and finally estimating the amount of labor required to build the cabinets. The other method is known as unit pricing and consists of determining, from past experience, the cost per linear foot of cabinet and then using that figure to prepare an estimate.

DETAILED QUANTITY-TAKEOFF ESTIMATES

Let's briefly examine the two systems. The detailed quantity-takeoff system involves making a list of all of the materials required to build the cabinets. A form such as the one shown in Table 14-2 may be used to list materials. After all the materials have been listed, they must be priced. Most shops keep catalogs from several material suppliers. If these are current, they may be used for most pricing. If a job requires a large quantity of a particular material, it is best to call the supplier to make sure the price is current. This is especially important during times of rapid inflation. You may also be able to get a lower

Table 14-2 A convenient form that can be used for quantity take-off and pricing of cabinet materials

		Quantity	Unit Price	Total
	For_____			
Wood Products				
¾-in. hardwood ply............................				
½-in. hardwood ply............................				
⅜-in. hardwood ply............................				
¼-in. hardwood ply............................				
¾-in. particle board..........................				
¾-in cabinet liner............................				
Hardwood lumber.............................				
½-in. drawer side mat				
Doors, drawer fronts				
¼-in. fir ply				
½-in. fir ply				
¾-in. fir ply				
_____				
_____				
Hardware				
Hinges......................................				
Pulls.......................................				
Knobs				
Catches.....................................				
Drawer slides				
Drawer roller guides.........................				
Lazy Susans				
Sink front trays				
Sink front hinges............................				
Adjustable shelf std.				
Shelf standard clips				
Screws				
Bolts				
Nails, staples				
_____				
_____				
_____				

	Quantity	Unit Price	Total
Finish			
Stain			
Sealer			
Lacquer.			
Penetrating oil			
Countertop			
Plastic laminate			
Contact cement			
Edge mold.			
Cove mold.			

price quote on a large quantity of material. Once all materials are priced, the total price for materials can be obtained.

The labor costs in building the cabinets are more difficult to determine. Records from past similar jobs provide the best basis for a time estimate on future jobs. The shop should use time cards to record the total amount of time that is required for each job. A rough estimate may be obtained by dividing the number of hours worked by the number of linear feet of cabinet. For example, a job that had 20 lin. ft. of cabinet and took 40 hr. to complete required 2 hr., on the average, to build each foot of cabinet. This is only a rough estimate, however, since it would probably take longer to build a base cabinet than an upper cabinet, longer to build a cabinet with drawers than one with shelves, and longer to build a corner cabinet than a straight one. A more accurate time estimate can be made on the basis of various units of work, such as making a drawer or installing a Lazy Susan. The best estimate of the amount of time required for an operation is based on accurate records of the time required for similar operations in the past. This method of estimating is the most accurate and is the one that should be used in most bidding situations.

UNIT PRICE ESTIMATES

The unit pricing method is less accurate but faster and may be useful in giving customers a rough price estimate. This data is also derived from previous jobs by keeping track of the cost of each job and dividing by the number of linear feet of cabinet in the job. If a job was done for $2,800 and had 32 lin. ft. of cabinets, the cost per linear foot was $87.50 ($2800 ÷ 32 = $87.50). It would obviously be very risky to bid a job based strictly on the linear footage of cabinet to be built. There are many variables, such as type of material and hardware and other features, that could cause the cost to vary considerably. If the unit method of pricing is to be used at all, it should be used in the same way that it is used to price new automobiles. The base car costs a certain amount, and the various optional features, such as power steering and air conditioning, are included at extra cost if the customer wants them.

Thus, it would be best to establish a base price per linear foot of base or wall cabinet. If the customer wanted roll-out trays, rather than fixed shelves, they would cost so much each; a Lazy Susan would cost so much; and so on. If the cabinets are built of cherry, that would add a certain amount to the base price. In this way, a quick estimate can be obtained by multiplying the number of linear feet of cabinet by the base rate and adding the cost of any special features. Even if you are not using the unit pricing method for estimating and bidding, it is a good idea to calculate the price per linear foot of your cabinets to compare them with figures found in some of the building-cost file books. These books are published yearly or, in some cases, quarterly and give unit prices of all components that make up a building. They are used by general contractors and architects to estimate building costs. They usually price cabinets on a linear-foot basis. By comparing your prices with those in these cost files, you can see how your costs compare with the average.

READING ARCHITECTURAL DRAWINGS AND SPECIFICATIONS

Before a bid can be prepared, you must determine exactly what the cabinet shop is to supply and how it must be built. This information is found in the architectural drawings (blueprints) and specifications, often referred to as the construction documents. The specifications are in book form and are usually organized according to the following standard format:

Division 1	General Requirements	Division 9	Finishes
Division 2	Site Work	Division 10	Specialties
Division 3	Concrete	Division 11	Equipment
Division 4	Masonry	Division 12	Furnishings
Division 5	Metals	Division 13	Special Construction
Division 6	Wood and Plastics	Division 14	Conveying Systems
Division 7	Thermal and Moisture Protection	Division 15	Mechanical
		Division 16	Electrical
Division 8	Doors and Windows		

Each division will have several sections and may include general provisions, materials, performance, and alternates. Most of the work supplied by the cabinetmaker is found in Division 6, Wood and Plastics.

If the cabinet shop is to also furnish the cabinets, Division 9 should be studied to obtain the finishing requirements.

The architectural drawings as described in Chapter 5 and the specifications tell the cabinetmaker what types of cabinets are to be built and what materials are to be used.

SUBMITTING THE BID

The bid is an agreement to provide cabinets and other woodwork as set forth in the construction documents for a fixed amount of money. It is, therefore, important that the subcontractor (in this case, the cabinetmaker) and the general contractor have an understanding of exactly what is to be supplied by the subcontractor.

The bid price should be submitted in writing and signed by an official of the company submitting the bid. The bid should state specifically what is to be supplied. Any alternatives should also be bid. For example, the base bid may be for birch cabinets, with an alternate quote requested for oak; or the base bid may be for plain plywood doors, with an alternate quote requested for frame-and-panel doors.

Standard contractor-subcontractor agreement forms are available, and these may be used to define the work involved, the time involved, and the manner of payment.

The subcontractor may be required to provide bid security in the form of bonding. This means that a bonding company guarantees the general contractor that you, the subcontractor, will perform the work that you have agreed to do. This protects the general contractor. If the subcontractor were to go broke and be unable to supply the cabinets as bid, the general contractor might not be able to find another shop on short notice to construct the required cabinets on time and at the bid price. The bonding company would cover any loss that the contractor sustains because of the delay.

GETTING INVITED TO BID

It is of no use to be skilled in building cabinets and in preparing bids if no one invites you to bid on projects. You have to inform contractors of your business and convince them that your company has the resources to provide the quality and quantity of cabinets that they may need. This may involve sending out printed advertising, showing them samples of your work, or providing names of past customers as references. You must get your name on their bid list so that you are included when they request bids on cabinetwork.

If you are interested in working directly with customers on residential work, you will need to advertise in local newspapers, on the radio, and elsewhere. Many communities have home shows. A booth at such a show, with a display of your cabinets, is a good way to show the public your work.

Index

A

Abrasives:
    grit sizes, 48
    for sanding cabinets, 185
    types, 48
Adhesives:
    for joining wood, 37–38
    for plastic laminates, 38, 225, 228
Air compressor, 202
Airless spraying, 204
Air pressure regulator, 202
Aliphatic resin glue, 37
Alternate bids, 241
Aluminum oxide paper, 48
American Plywood Association, 32
Animal hide glue, 38
Annual growth rings, 17
Architects scale, 58–69, 74
Architectural drawings, 65–66, 240–41
Ash (wood), 27
Assembly:
    cabinet, 173–84, 188–93
    doors, 121–24
    drawers, 136–38
    face frame, 99–101
Auxiliary fence for table saw, 150
Auxiliary table for table saw, 150

B

Backs:
    base cabinet, 177
    drawer, 130, 137
    wall cabinet, 192
Back splash, 232–33
Banding, edge:
    plastic laminates, 225–27
    shelves, 182, 193
Band saw, 171
Bark, tree, 16–17
Bath cabinets, 63
Belt sander:
    portable, 125, 185–86
    wide, 100–101, 124–25
Bevel cuts:
    making dovetail joint, 131, 135
    plastic laminate trimming, 230
    for raised panel, 119–21
Bidding cabinet jobs, 235, 241
Birch, 24–25
Bits:
    plastic laminate trimming, 226–27, 230
    router, 166
Black walnut, 24, 26
Blades:

panel raising, 119
spindle shaper, 163
table saw (plywood cutting), 110
Blueprint, 65, 240
Board feet, 31
Bonding (*see* Adhesives)
Bonding—bid, 241
Book matched veneer, 34
Brushes, paint, 201–2
Burn-in, repair method, 196
Butt joint:
    base cabinet, 91
    face frame, 54

C

Cabinetmaking, 1–2
Cambium, 16–17
Casein, glue, 38
Casing nails, 39
Cell structure of wood, 16, 18
Center guide, drawer, 138–42
Checks in lumber, 15, 19–20
Cherry, 27
Chip breaker, router fence, 167
Chisel mortiser, 92–93
Clamping:
    cabinets, 181, 184
    doors, 122–23
    face frames, 99–101
    fixture for clamping doors, 123
Clamp nails, 124
Closed coat abrasive, 48
Cloth, abrasive backing, 48
Coated abrasives, 48
Collars, depth for spindle shaper, 118–19, 165
Coloring:
    chemical, 198
    stains, 197–99
Commercial drawer guides, 45–46, 143-44
Compressor, air, 202
Contact cement, 38, 225, 228
Contour routing, 164–65, 169
Contour shaping, 117–19, 164–66
Contractor:
    general, 235, 241
    sub, 241
Cope joint, 114–15
Cores, plywood, 33
Corner cabinets, 12, 60–63
Cost estimating, 237–40
Costs:
    labor, 239
    materials, 237–39

overhead, 235–37
Cross cutting:
 with the radial arm saw, 90
 with the table saw, 90
Curing, glue, 37
Cutters:
 panel raising, 119
 shaper, 163
Cutting:
 cabinet parts, 153–61
 dado, 159
 dovetail, 131–33
 edge banding, 162
 face frame parts, 88–90
 grooves for shelf standard, 160
 large sheet materials, 110–12,
  150–53
 miter, 157, 160
 moldings, 162–69
 mortise, 92–93
 plastic laminates, 223–24
 pull board cut out, 95–99
 rabbet, 158
 raised panel with table saw, 119–21
 sink cut out, 230–31
 tenon, 92, 94–95
 toe kick for base cabinet, 157
Cutting list, 78–84

D

Dado:
 double, drawers, 131, 133–35
 dovetail, 131–33
 machining, 159
Danish oil finish, 201
Deciduous trees, 16
Depreciation of equipment, 235–36
Detail drawings, 66–67
Detailed quantity take-off, 237–39
Diamond matching (veneer), 34
Dimensions:
 cabinet drawings, 78
 dressed lumber (table), 30
 typical cabinet, 51
Dishwasher space, 60
Door(s):
 assembly, 121–24
 construction details, 114–21
 hardware, 41–45
 hinge locating jig, 189
 installation, 188
 lipping, 112–13
 raised panel, 119–21
Double dado joint, 131, 133–35
Dovetail, 131–32

Dovetail dado, 131–33
Dowel joint, 54
Drafting equipment, 68–70
Drawer:
 assembly, 136–38
 construction, 130–31
 design, 129–31
 guide systems, 138–44
 installation, 138–42, 187–88
 joints, 131–35
 materials, 130
 roller guides, 45–46, 143–44
 types, 129–30
Drawing cabinets, 68–78
Drawing layout, 68–71
Drying lumber, 18–21

E

Early wood (spring growth), 17
Edge band:
 cutting, 162
 plastic laminate, 225–27
 shelves, 193
Edge gluing, 22
Edge jointing, 87–88
Edge molding, 162–69
Elevation view, 65–66
End shaping, 164–65
Epoxy resin, 38
Estimating labor, 239
Estimating material, 237–40
Expansion of wood, 18–21
Extension lines (drawing), 75–77
Extension table (table saw), 150
External mix paint gun, 204
Eye protection, 169

F

Face frame:
 assembly, 99–101
 construction, 85–98
 design, 52–56
 installation, 177, 181
 mullions, 52–53
 rails, 52–53
 stiles, 52–53
Face jointing boards, 86
Factory and shop lumber, 29
FAS (hardwood lumber grade), 30
Fasteners:
 clamp nails, 41
 nails, 38–39
 screws, 39
 staples, 40–41

Finishing:
  cabinets, 204–8
  equipment, 201–4
  materials, 197–201
  nails, 39
  preparation for, 196–97
  procedures, 204–8
Flat grained lumber (plain sawn), 28
Flat head screws, 39
Flint paper, 48
Flitch (veneers), 34
Floor plans (kitchens), 9–10
Flush doors, 104, 106
Flush drawers, 130
Formica, 36
Frame and panel doors, 106–9, 114–26
Free water, 20
Functional design, 6–10

G

Garnet paper, 48
General contractor, 235, 241
Glue, removing excess, 196
Glues, 37–38
Grading:
  of abrasive grits, 48
  of lumber, 29–30
  of plywood, 32
Grain:
  appearance on plain sawn vs. quarter
    sawn lumber, 28
  appearance on various veneer cuts, 33
Grit sizes (abrasives), 48
Grooves:
  adjustable shelf standard, 160
  drawer side guides, 140
  splines, 161
Growth rings, 17
Guards, 169–71
Guides:
  drawer, 45–46, 138–44
  pin for overarm router, 167, 169

H

Hanging doors, 188
Hardboard, 35
Hardness of wood, 16
Hardware, cabinet, 41–47
Hardwoods:
  defined, 16
  grades, 30
  plywood, 32–34
  specific species, 23–27
Haunched mortise and tenon, 92–94

Heartwood, 16–17
Hinge locating jig, 189
Hinges:
  demountable, 42–44
  flush doors, 43
  overlay doors, 41–42
  3/8 inset (lip) doors, 41–42
Hollow chisel mortiser, 92–93
Hot lacquer application, 199–200
Humidity, effect on wood, 18–23

I

Inner bark, 16–17
Installation:
  adjustable shelf standard, 191
  back splash, 232–33
  base cabinet, 211–219
  counter top, 217–19
  drawer guides, 138–44
  wall cabinet, 219–21
Interior plywood, 32
Internal mix spray gun, 204

J

Jointer, 86–88
Jointer safety rules, 170

K

Kick back, 170–171
Kicker, 138
Kiln drying, 23
Kitchen:
  functional design, 6–10
  layout, 9–10
  space requirements, 8–9
  work centers, 8
Knobs for drawers and doors, 44

L

Labor, estimating cost of, 239
Lacquer, 199–200
Laminated plastic:
  cutting, 223–24
  description of, 36–37
  installation of, 225–30
Laminated wood, 22
Layout for drawing, 68–71
Lazy Susan for corner cabinet, 12, 61–62
Lip doors, 103–4
  hardware, 41–42
  installation, 188
L-shaped kitchen, 9–10

Lumber:
    board foot calculation, 31
    cutting methods, 28
    defects, 15, 29–30
    drying, 23
    grading, 29–30
    kiln-dried, 23
    kinds of, 23–27
    shrinkage, 18–21
    sizes, 30
Lumber core plywood, 33

M

Machine safety, 169–71
Magnetic catch, 44
Mahogany, Philippine, 24–25
Maple, 24, 26
Matching veneers, 34–35
Materials, estimating cost of, 237–39
Measuring for cabinet installation, 67–68
Medium density fiberboard, 36
Medullary rays, 17–18
Minimum space requirements for
    cabinets, 8–9
Miter:
    for cabinet base, 157
    finished end to finished back, 160
Moisture content of wood, 19–20
Moisture meter, 19
Moldings:
    blades for cutting, 163
    cutting on overhead router, 167–69
    cutting on shaper, 164
    cutting with portable router, 164–67
    metal for plastic laminates, 232–33
Mortise and tenon joint, 52–53, 92–95
Mortiser, 92–93
Mortising, 92–93
Mullions, 52–53

N

Nailing strip, 51–52, 177–78, 192
Nailing with pneumatic nailer, 173–74
Nail sizes, 39
Nominal dimensions of lumber, 30
Non-grain raising stains, 198
Notation of drawings, 77–78

O

Oak, red, 24–25
Oak, white, 24–25
Ogee sticking, 114
Oil finish, 201

Oil stains, 197–98
Oleoresinous varnish, 200
Open coat abrasives, 48
Open grain woods, finishing, 199
Outer bark, 16–17
Oval head screws, 39
Oven cabinet, 56–57
Overarm router, 167–69
Overhead, business expense, 235–37

P

Panel door, 3, 7, 106–9, 114–26
Panel raising cutter, 119
Paper for abrasives, 48
Particle board, 35
Partitions, cabinet, 52, 158, 176
Paste fillers, 199
Penetrating oil finishes, 201
Penny (nail sizes), 39
Philippine Mahogany, 24–25
Pigment oil stains, 197–98
Pin guide for overarm router, 167, 169
Pivot hinge, 41
Plain sawn lumber, 28
Plain sliced veneer, 33
Planer, 86–87, 171
Planing face frame material, 86–87
Planning kitchen layout, 6–10
Plastic laminates:
    cutting, 223–24
    description, 36
Plastic resin glue, 38
Plywood:
    cutting, 110–12, 150–53
    description, 31
    grading, 32
    lumber core, 33
    particle board core, 33
    veneer core, 33
    veneers, 33
Pneumatic nailers and staplers, 40–41,
    173–74
Pocket cut (in face frame for pull board),
    95–99
Polymerization, 201
Polyurethane, 200
Polyvinyl resin glue, 37
Pores in wood, 18
Portable nailers (see Pneumatic nailers
    and staplers)
Portable router, 164–67
Portable sanders, 125–26, 185–86
Pressure feed spray gun, 203–4
Profit, estimating, 237
Properties of selected hardwoods, 23–27

Pulls for drawers and doors, 44
Pumice, 201
Push block, 86
Push stick, 89

Q

Quantity take off, estimating, 237–39
Quarter sawn lumber, 28
Quarter sliced veneer, 33

R

Rabbet, cutting on:
  router table, 113
  shaper, 113
  table saw, 158–59
Rabbet joints:
  for cabinets, 59, 159
  for doors, 112
  for drawers, 131
Radial arm saw, 90, 156
Rails:
  door, 106–7
  drawer guide, 138
  face frame, 52–53
Raised panel, 107, 114, 119–21
Rays (medullary), 17–18
Red oak, 24–25
Refrigerator cabinet, 58–59
Repairing defects in wood, 196
Resorcinol resin glue, 38
Reverse diamond match (veneer), 34–35
Rings, growth, 17
Ripping:
  narrow stock, 89
  plywood, 152
  solid lumber, 88–89
Rotary veneer cutting, 33
Rottenstone, 201
Round head wood screws, 39
Router:
  cutting moldings, 164–67
  overarm, 167–69
Rubbing, 201

S

Saber saw, 99
Safety:
  band saw, 170
  jointer, 170
  planer, 170
  pneumatic nailers, 173–74
  radial arm saw, 170
  shaper, 170

  table saw, 89, 170
Sanders:
  finish, 125–26, 185–86
  portable belt, 125–26, 185–86
  wide belt, 100–101, 124–25
Sanding:
  assembled cabinet, 185–87
  doors, 124–26
  face frame, 100–101
Sanding sealer, 199, 209
Sapwood, 16–17
Saw:
  blades, 110
  radial arm, 90, 156
  saber, 99
  table, 110–12, 147–57
Sawing:
  plywood and sheet materials, 110–12,
    147–57
  safety, 89, 170
  solid lumber, 88–89
Scale, architects, 68–69, 74
Scale for setting rip fence, 148–49
Screws, wood, 39
Sealer, 199
Shaper, 114–15
  curved moldings, 164–66
  cutting moldings, 162–66
  cutting rabbets, 113
  safety, 170
  sliding, 127
  styles, 106–9
  symbols for, 65, 75, 77
  tambour, 127–28
Sheet abrasives, 48
Shellac, 200
Shelves:
  adjustable, 59–60, 160, 191
  hardware, 59–60, 191
  installation, 174, 177
Shims, for installing cabinets, 212, 216
Shrinkage of wood, 18–21
Side guides, drawer, 140, 143
Silicon carbide abrasive paper, 48
Single end tenoner, 92, 94
Sink:
  cabinet, 8, 56
  cut out, 230–31
  plumbing, 217
Siphon feed spray gun (*see* Suction feed
    spray gun)
Sliding doors, 127
Slip matched veneer, 34
Softwood:
  defined, 16
  grading system, 29–30
  plywood, 31–34

sizes, 32
Spacer collar shaper, 164–65
Special purpose cabinets, 60–63
Specifications (construction documents),
    66, 240–41
Spindle shaper, 162–66, 170
Spline, 161
Spray finishing:
    equipment, 202–4
    technique, 204–8
Spring wood, 17
Squaring stock, 86–87
Staining products, 197–99
Standard hardboard, 35
Standards:
    adjustable shelf, 59–60
    Architectural Woodwork Institute, 85,
        173
    cabinet space, 8–9
Stapler, pneumatic, 40–41, 173–74
Stapling, 173–74
Starting pin, shaper, 164, 166
Sticking, 114
Stiles:
    doors, 106–7
    face frame, 52–53
Stop block, 156
Styles of:
    cabinets, 3
    doors, 106–9
Subcontractor, 241
Submitting bids, 241
Suction feed spray gun, 203
Summer wood, 17
Supports, adjustable shelf, 59–60
Surface planer (surfacer), 86–87, 171
Symbols for doors, 65, 75, 77
Synthetic finishes, 200

T

Table, offbearing for table saw, 150
Table saw, 89, 110–12, 147–57
Tack rag, 197
Tambour doors, 127–28
Tempered hardboard, 35
Tenon, 52–53, 92, 94–95
Tenoner, 94
Three-wing shaper cutter, 163
Toe space on cabinets, 53, 157
Top coats, finishing, 199–201

Track for doors, 127–28
Tree cross section, 17
Trim, aluminum for plastic laminate,
    232–33
T-square, 68–69

U

Unit price estimates, 239–40
U-shaped kitchen, 10
Utilities, costs, 236

V

Varnish, 200
V-block for holding shelves, 193
Veneer:
    cutting methods, 33
    matching, 34–35
    for plywood, 32–34
    plywood core, 32–33
Vertical grade plastic laminate, 36
Vertical grain lumber (quarter sawn), 28

W

Walls (*see* Measuring for cabinet
    installation)
Walnut, 24, 26
Warp, 20
Water in wood, 18–21
Waterproof abrasive paper, 48
Water stains, 197
Wax, 147, 200–201
White ash, 27
White glue, 37
White oak, 24–25
Wide belt sander, 100–101, 124–25
Wood:
    cell structure, 18
    composition, 16–18
    defects, 29
    kinds of, 23–27
    moisture content, 18–21
    shrinkage, 18–21
Wood lacquer, 199–200

Y

Yard lumber, 29